THE NO SMOKE AND MIRRORS WORKBOOK:

Overcome the Financial Myths That Will Ruin Your Retirement Dreams

David Trahair, CA

Self-Counsel Press
(*a division of*)
International Self-Counsel Press Ltd.
Canada   USA

*Self-Counsel Press acknowledges the financial support of the Government of Canada
through the Book Publishing Industry Development Program (BPIDP) for our publishing ac-
tivities.*

Printed in Canada.

First edition: 2006

Library and Archives Canada Cataloguing in Publication

Trahair, David
   The no smoke and mirrors workbook : overcome the financial myths that will
ruin your retirement dreams / David Trahair.

Accompanied by a CD-ROM.
Supplement to: author's Smoke & mirrors 3rd ed.
ISBN 1-55180-692-4

   1. Finance, Personal--Canada. 2. Retirement income--Canada. 3. Investments--
Canada. I. Trahair, David Smoke & mirrors. II. Title.

HG179.T722 2005a Suppl.   332.024'014'0971   C2005-906597-4

Self-Counsel Press
(a division of)
International Self-Counsel Press Ltd.
1481 Charlotte Road   1704 North State Street
North Vancouver, BC V7J 1H1   Bellingham, WA 98225
Canada   USA

CONTENTS

NOTICE TO READERS

The author, the publisher, and the vendor of this book make no representations or warranties regarding the outcome or the use to which the information in this book is put and are not assuming any liability for any claims, losses, or damages arising out of the use of this book. The reader should not rely on the author or publisher of this book for any professional advice. Please be sure that you have the most recent edition.

INTRODUCTION

This workbook is meant to accompany my book *Smoke and Mirrors: Financial Myths That Will Ruin Your Retirement Dreams.* If you've read the book and want to apply the concepts to your own life, this is for you.

Though many people are concerned about the state of their family finances, very few actually do something about it. But by reading this workbook and working your way through the accompanying spreadsheets, you will have taken a major step towards getting control of your personal finances.

It's not necessary to take on the whole project at once. In fact, the best way is to take one step at a time. But even if you never get to all the steps, working through just one of them could make a huge difference to your family's financial future.

Take your RRSP for example. Say you go through the step to determine how well your investment adviser has been doing and, as a result, discover that your RRSP investments are actually worth less than the dollars you've put in. If you continue with this adviser, you are literally throwing away perhaps tens of thousands of your hard-earned dollars. Working through that step has given you the information you need to make a decision.

That's the key here. Going through these exercises may lead you to plug at least one money drain. The alternative is to continue doing what you are doing now. Can you really afford that?

About This Workbook

This workbook is structured in a sequence of practical steps that I recommend you take to gain control of your finances. The spreadsheets that accompany each step are designed to perform calculations that will provide you with need-to-know information about your financial situation. They are filled out with practical examples illustrating each step. I'm hoping you will read through this workbook once and then take control and enter your own figures into the spreadsheets. If a step doesn't apply to you, just skip it. You can always return to it when it does.

Here are the five steps, including the Microsoft Excel spreadsheets we'll be using in each:

Step 1: **Calculating Your Net Worth**

My Net Worth Calculator

Step 2: **Optimizing Your Retirement**

The Retirement Optimizer

Step 3: **The Great Debate: RRSP versus Paying Off Debt**

The Personal Rate of Return Calculator

RRSP Value Projector for Mortgage at Retirement

Coffee-skipping Way to Retirement Projector

Step 4: **Detailed Personal Financial Tracking**

Money Drain Pain

My Income and Expenses

Cash Flow Projector

Step 5: Cars: Should I Lease or Buy?

Car Lease versus Buy Analyzer

If you work your way systematically through each spreadsheet as it applies to you, by the time you reach the end of this workbook you'll have a clear picture of your finances and know what you need to do to have the kind of retirement you want.

About the Spreadsheets

All the spreadsheets come on the CD-ROM that is included with this package. Unlike the spreadsheets that come with *Smoke and Mirrors: Financial Myths That Will Ruin Your Retirement Dreams*, these spreadsheets are totally unprotected, meaning you can change and customize them as you see fit. I have also unhidden all the tabs so you can change things like tax rates as needed. However, the downside of unprotected spreadsheets is that you could accidentally delete some important formulas, so I strongly recommend that you make a copy of each spreadsheet to work on and leave the originals intact.

I have tried to make the spreadsheets easy to use but I realize some of you may not be too comfortable with Excel. I have included Excel "Tips" throughout this workbook to help you understand the formulas and possibly use them elsewhere.

Some of the spreadsheets that come on the CD-ROM are blank, and some will have sample data filled in that match the printed examples in this workbook. If the spreadsheet you are using has an example already filled in, simply type over the sample data with your own.

Each square on a spreadsheet is called a cell. You'll also note that the examples are printed with the column and row headings visible. Columns are labelled A, B, C, etc., and rows 1, 2, 3, etc. Column and row headings can be used to identify a specific cell. For instance, the cell that is in the second row in the second column is called cell B2. By using column and row headings, I can refer you to a specific cell in the detailed step-by-step text that accompanies each spreadsheet.

EXCEL TIP

If you prefer not to have the row (1,2,3, etc.) and column (A,B,C, etc.) headings on your printouts, follow these steps:

Select "File" from the top menu,

then "Page Setup,"

then "Sheet."

Then un-tick the box to the left of "Row and column headings."

Let's get started.

Step 1

CALCULATING YOUR NET WORTH

If you want to get control of your money and start to make real progress toward a comfortable retirement, you need to start by calculating your net worth.

A net worth statement is simply a summary of the things you own ("assets" such as cash, RRSPs, your house) less the amounts you owe ("liabilities" or debts such as mortgages, car loans, lines of credit, and credit card balances). The total of your assets less your debts is your net worth. If you're familiar with business terms, think of your net worth statement as your personal balance sheet; or if accounting is not your thing, think of it as your personal financial scorecard.

A net worth calculation helps you understand where you stand financially. It's the measure of how well you have done to date with your personal finances.

Most people never calculate their net worth. Why? Because they don't have to. But the sooner you do this for yourself, the sooner you'll know exactly what your financial situation is, and the easier it will be to change it. Don't put it off. The closer you get to retirement, the less time you have to make significant improvements.

Let's get started with our first example. If you open the My Net Worth Calculator spreadsheet on your computer, you'll see that it is divided into three "tabs." Those are the labels at the bottom left of the page: "Home," "Questions," and "Results." The Home page displayed in Figure 1-1 shows the version number in cell B2 and also has links to the other two tabs in cells B12 and B13. There is also a link to my website, <www.smokeandmirrors .ca>, in cell B16.

FIGURE 1-1

	A	B	C	D	E	F	G	H	I	J
1	**My Net Worth Calculator**									
2	Version	92105								
3										
4	Welcome, and don't worry. You don't have to be an Excel expert to use this spreadsheet!									
5										
6	All you need to do is answer the questions on the Questions tab and then go to the Results tab to find:									
7		A summary of what you own (assets)								
8		A summary of what you owe (debts or liablities)								
9		How much you are worth								
10										
11	**INDEX (Click the words to go to the worksheets or click on the tabs below.)**									
12		Questions								
13		Results								
14										
15	If you would like further information about how to simplify your finances, come and visit us at:									
16		Smokeandmirrors.ca								
17										
18	© Copyright 2005/2006 David Trahair, CA									

EXCEL TIP

Each Excel file is really a workbook that is a collection of tabs or "worksheets." When you open a new blank file in Excel it will usually have three blank tabs at the bottom labelled "Sheet1," "Sheet2," and "Sheet3" by default. You can change the name of the tabs by right-clicking the mouse and selecting "Rename." You can also create a new tab by right-clicking the mouse on any tab, selecting "Insert...," and then selecting "Worksheet."

The Questions Tab

Have a look at Figure 1-2 on the following page. Alternatively, if you open the My Net Worth Calculator spreadsheet on your computer and click on the link to the Questions tab or click on the tab itself at the bottom of the sheet, you will be taken to another sheet where you'll see a list of questions in one column and the corresponding answers in a second column. These questions are designed to step anyone through itemizing his or her assets and liabilities.

FIGURE 1-2

	A	B	C	D	E	F	G	H	I	J	K	L
1	**My Net Worth Calculator Questions**											
2												Your
3	Answer these questions in column L:											Answers
4												
5	1 What date are you calculating your net worth at?											12/31/2005
6	(e.g., 12/31/2005 or 31/12/2005)											
7												
8	2 What is your first and last name?											Joe Test
9	(e.g., Joe Test)											
10												
11	3 How much is in your chequing account on your most recent statement?											$1,000.00
12												
13	4 How much is in your savings account on your most recent statement?											$350.00
14												
15	5 What is the value of your home (principal residence) if you own one?											$300,000.00
16	(If you don't own one, enter 0.)											
17												
18	6 What is the value of your cottage or vacation property if you own one?											$150,000.00
19	(If you don't own one, enter 0.)											
20												
21	7 How much is your main car worth if you own one?											$25,000.00
22	(Note: If you lease a car, **don't** enter a value since you don't own it.)											
23												
24	8 How much is your second car worth if you own one?											$6,000.00
25												
26	9 If you own a small business, what do you estimate its worth to be?											$50,000.00
27												
28	10 What is the total value of your investments **outside** an RRSP, if any?											$35,000.00
29												
30	11 What is the total market value of your RESPs on the most recent statement?											$2,000.00
31												
32	12 What is the total market value of your RRSPs on the most recent statement?											$100,000.00
33												
34	13 What is the total market value of your **spouse's** RRSPs on the most recent statement?											$75,000.00
35												
36	14 What is the current balance owing on your main credit card?											$3,500.00
37												
38	15 What is the current balance owing on your other credit cards?											$500.00
39												
40	16 What is the current balance owing on your line(s) of credit?											$38,000.00
41												
42	17 What is the current amount owing on your home mortgage?											$190,000.00
43												
44	18 What is the current amount owing on your cottage mortgage, if any?											$80,000.00
45												
46	19 How much do you owe on your main car loan, if any?											$12,000.00
47												
48	20 How much do you owe on your second car loan, if any?											$0.00
49												
50	21 If you owe taxes from prior years, enter the amount here.											$0.00

You'll see that our subject, Joe Test, has entered in Column L his answers to the questions. In this sample, the answer to the question about the net worth date is "12/31/05." (Note that in Canada, the convention is to show the date as Month/Day/Year rather than Day/Month/Year. The date format can be changed in your Microsoft Windows Settings. Go to "Control Panel" and choose "Regional and Language Options." Make sure you're on the "Regional Options" tab, click on "Customize," and then the "Date" tab.)

The Results Tab

Have a look at Figure 1-3, or if you're looking at the spreadsheet on your computer, go to the Results tab by clicking on the tab. (You'll be taken to a sheet that looks just like a financial statement.)

The program has entered the amounts from the Questions tab into the appropriate cells on the Results tab. It has also added and subtotalled the amounts.

Joe has total cash and bank accounts of $1,350, other assets (house, cottage, and cars) worth $481,000, and investments (business, RESP, RRSPs, etc.) totalling $262,000. His total assets are worth $744,350, which is the sum of all three subtotals.

Scroll down to his liabilities (click on the down arrow key on the bottom right side of the spreadsheet). He owes $42,000 on credit cards and lines of credit and $282,000 on mortgages and other loans, for total debt of $324,000.

To obtain his net worth, the program has taken his total assets of $744,350 and subtracted from that figure his total liabilities of $324,000. The result — $420,350 — is Joe's net worth as at December 31, 2005.

FIGURE 1-3

	A	B	C	D	E	F
1	**My Net Worth Calculator Results for:**					**Joe Test**
2						
3	**Net Worth Calculation Date:**					**12/31/2005**
4						
5	**MY NET WORTH STATEMENT**					
6						
7	**ASSETS**					**$**
8	**Cash and Bank Accounts**					
9	Chequing account					1,000.00
10	Savings account					350.00
11	**Total cash and bank accounts**					**1,350.00**
12						
13	**Other Assets (market value)**					
14	Principal residence					300,000.00
15	Cottage					150,000.00
16	Main car					25,000.00
17	Second car					6,000.00
18	**Total other assets**					**481,000.00**
19						
20	**Investments (market value)**					
21	Business value					50,000.00
22	Investments outside RRSP					35,000.00
23	RESP					2,000.00
24	RRSP					100,000.00
25	RRSP — Spouse					75,000.00
26	**Total investments**					**262,000.00**
27						
28	**TOTAL ASSETS**					**744,350.00**
29						
30	**LIABILITIES**					
31	**Credit Cards and Lines of Credit**					
32	Main credit card					3,500.00
33	Other credit cards					500.00
34	Lines of credit					38,000.00
35	**Total credit cards and lines of credit**					**42,000.00**
36						
37	**Other Liabilities**					
38	Principal residence mortgage					190,000.00
39	Cottage mortgage					80,000.00
40	Main car loan					12,000.00
41	Second car loan					0.00
42	Prior year personal taxes					0.00
43	**Total other liabilities**					**282,000.00**
44						
45	**TOTAL LIABILITIES**					**324,000.00**
46						
47	**NET WORTH (Assets - Liabilities)**					**420,350.00**

Try It with Your Own Numbers

Now try it with your own numbers … and start making some progress. Gather all your most recent financial statements (bank accounts, mortgages, investments, RRSPs, RESPs) along with all your credit card bills and loan statements and start plugging your numbers into Column L of the Questions tab. You can enter your information right over the sample data in each cell. (Note that all figures should be entered as positive. There is no need to put a minus sign in front of debts or liabilities. The program automatically accounts for liabilities as negative.)

If you're in a relationship with a significant other (or married), create a combined net worth statement because you will likely have joint ownership of many things such as houses, cars, and bank accounts.

Once you're done, go to the Results tab. You can now see exactly where you stand financially.

EXCEL TIP

It's easy to create a formula to do a simple sum. The formula to add up a column of numbers from, say, cell A1 to cell D1 is:

$$=SUM(A1:D1)$$

Getting Ahead Is Like a Hockey Game

You should do a net worth statement each year. It's the best and easiest way to see for certain how well you're doing — whether you're gaining or losing on your personal financial scorecard.

Since we're talking about scorecards, let's make a sports analogy to clarify the point. Compare your battle to achieve a stress-free, comfortable retirement to a hockey game. The game has three periods, and the objective is to outscore your opponent by the end of the game.

That's what gaining control of your money is like, isn't it? It's a constant battle against a strong opponent. In this case, the other team has many players: the difficulty of spending less than you make, unscrupulous investment advisers, bad investment decisions, etc. It's not going to be easy but it's the fight of your financial life.

EXCEL TIP

If you have assets or liabilities not listed on the Net Worth Calculator spreadsheet, don't worry. You can simply insert lines where needed. That's the beauty of Excel.

Say you have a boat at the cottage that you bought for $12,000. Don't bother typing the question on the Questions tab. Simply go to the Results tab and click on cell A16 ("Main Car" under "Cottage"), select "Insert" from the top menu, and then select "Rows."

Excel will insert the row and move everything else down one row. Enter "12,000" in cell F16. Notice that Excel has automatically recalculated the result for "Total other assets" and also adjusted all other affected equations.

Your net worth statement is like the scoreboard. It will always tell you how well you are doing in the game. Ignoring your net worth statement is like playing a game without bothering to check what the score is. It's tough to win when you have no idea where you stand!

What about bad periods? Even if you are very disciplined and have your earnings, investments, and spending well under control, there will probably be times when it seems the opposition is winning. Those unexpected expenses (such as a new roof!) will often blindside you. Try not to worry too much about it. Those things will happen, and you are going to have some tough periods.

As in hockey, however, the key is to never give up. Your retirement comfort depends on it!

Step 2

OPTIMIZING YOUR RETIREMENT

If you want to discover the most efficient way to achieve a comfortable retirement for yourself, begin with the end in mind. How much money will you actually need once you stop working? What's the point of slaving away day after dreary day at a job you don't like, making sacrifices to max out your RRSP contributions and build a huge nest egg that you'll never use? No one wants to run out of money in retirement, but by the same token, you don't need to save much more than you can reasonably spend over the rest of your life.

Don't get me wrong here. I am not saying, "Forget RRSPs. You won't need them." However, I am asking you to think about how large your RRSP realistically needs to be for you to live comfortably in retirement. Once you know that, you can make an informed decision about the trade-off between living well today and enjoying life and time with your loved ones against the risk of being short of money during your retirement.

But what does optimizing your retirement really mean? It means growing your RRSP so that it is big enough to provide enough cash to pay your expenses, but not so big that you are forced to withdraw and pay tax on more money than you need — as well as ending up with excess income that causes a clawback of your Old Age Security pension. It means focusing your retirement-planning efforts from now on so that you can enjoy a worry-free retirement and never run out of money — and do so without living a miserable life scrimping by until your sunset years.

I created the Retirement Optimizer spreadsheet specifically to help you with this, and have made optimizing your retirement the second step in this workbook because it impacts almost everything else in your personal financial decision making.

For example, the question of whether it's better for you to invest in RRSPs versus paying off debt is much easier to answer if you have an idea about how big your RRSP needs to be when you retire. Optimizing your RRSP requires you to determine how big it needs to be.

Here's another way you may wish to optimize your retirement: If you are knowledgeable about real estate, perhaps it makes sense to invest in it rather than further inflate your RRSP. By doing do, you could end up with large gains taxed favourably (as these would be capital gains, which currently are only 50 percent taxable). You'd also have the huge benefit of timing your own dispositions and therefore controlling the amount of tax you pay. In other words, maybe it makes better sense to invest in assets outside your RRSP, sell them only when you need the cash, and pay less tax on the resulting gains.

With that in mind, it's time to move to the Retirement Optimizer spreadsheet. By spending just a little time filling out this spreadsheet, you can get a clear picture of just how much money you can expect to have in your retirement.

The Home Tab

Have a look at Figure 2-1. Alternatively, you can open the Retirement Optimizer spreadsheet on your computer. Just like the My Net Worth Calculator in Step 1, the Home tab on this spreadsheet contains some basic information about the spreadsheet and includes the version number (cell B2) and links to the five other tabs.

FIGURE 2-1

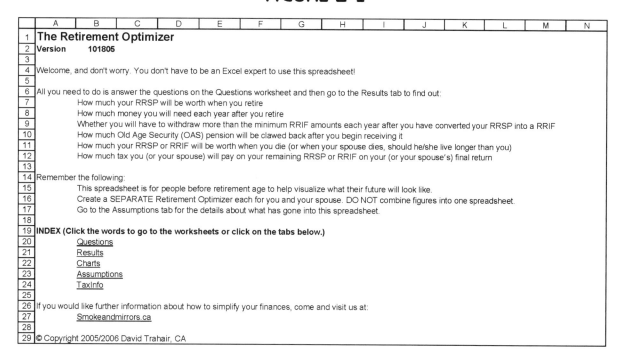

	A	B	C	D	E	F	G	H	I	J	K	L	M	N
1	**The Retirement Optimizer**													
2	Version	101805												
3														
4	Welcome, and don't worry. You don't have to be an Excel expert to use this spreadsheet!													
5														
6	All you need to do is answer the questions on the Questions worksheet and then go to the Results tab to find out:													
7		How much your RRSP will be worth when you retire												
8		How much money you will need each year after you retire												
9		Whether you will have to withdraw more than the minimum RRIF amounts each year after you have converted your RRSP into a RRIF												
10		How much Old Age Security (OAS) pension will be clawed back after you begin receiving it												
11		How much your RRSP or RRIF will be worth when you die (or when your spouse dies, should he/she live longer than you)												
12		How much tax you (or your spouse) will pay on your remaining RRSP or RRIF on your (or your spouse's) final return												
13														
14	Remember the following:													
15		This spreadsheet is for people before retirement age to help visualize what their future will look like.												
16		Create a SEPARATE Retirement Optimizer each for you and your spouse. DO NOT combine figures into one spreadsheet.												
17		Go to the Assumptions tab for the details about what has gone into this spreadsheet.												
18														
19	**INDEX (Click the words to go to the worksheets or click on the tabs below.)**													
20		Questions												
21		Results												
22		Charts												
23		Assumptions												
24		TaxInfo												
25														
26	If you would like further information about how to simplify your finances, come and visit us at:													
27		Smokeandmirrors.ca												
28														
29	© Copyright 2005/2006 David Trahair, CA													

The Questions Tab

Once again, we've used a sample subject, Joe Fifty, to illustrate how this spreadsheet works. Figure 2-2 on the following page shows the Questions tab of this spreadsheet. You'll see that the questions are all simple and straightforward and that they cover various aspects of retirement planning. You'll also see that Joe Fifty has entered his answers to those questions in the appropriate cells in Column L. When it comes time for you to fill out this spreadsheet with your own information, you'll do the same.

FIGURE 2-2

	A	B	C	D	E	F	G	H	I	J	K	L
1	**Retirement Optimizer Questions**											
2												**Your**
3	Answer these questions in Column L:											**Answers**
4												
5	**GENERAL**											
6	What is today's date?											**10/18/2005**
7	(e.g., 10/18/2005 or 18/10/2005)											
8												
9	What is your first and last name?											**Joe Fifty**
10	(e.g., Joe Test)											
11												
12	On what day were you born?											**1/2/1955**
13	(e.g., 10/25/1960 or 25/10/1960)											
14												
15	**RRSP/RRIF**											
16	What is the total market value of your RRSPs on the most recent statement?											**$95,000**
17												
18	How much do you plan to contribute to your RRSP each year from now until retirement?											**$5,000**
19												
20	At what age do you plan to retire and stop making RRSP contributions?											**65**
21												
22	At what annual rate of return do you expect your RRSP investments to grow **until** you retire?											**5.00%**
23												
24	At what annual rate of return do you expect your RRSP or RRIF investments to grow **after** you retire?											**4.00%**
25												
26	What average annual rate of inflation do you expect over the remainder of your life?											**2.00%**
27												
28	**OLD AGE SECURITY**											
29	Are you eligible for the maximum Old Age Security (OAS) pension at age 65? (Y=Yes, N=No)											**N**
30	(If you have lived in Canada for at least 40 years after turning 18, you will receive the maximum pension.)											
31												
32	If not, how many years will you have lived in Canada since your 18th birthday when you turn 65?											**30**
33	(You must have lived in Canada for at least 10 years to qualify for OAS.)											
34												
35	**CANADA PENSION PLAN**											
36	Are you eligible for the maximum Canada Pension Plan (CPP) pension at age 65? (Y=Yes, N=No)											**N**
37	(If on average from age 18 to retirement your earnings exceeded the maximum pensionable earnings											
38	($41,100 in 2005), you will receive the maximum CPP pension.)											
39												
40	If not, what has your average annual income from earnings been since you turned 18?											**$30,000**
41	(Enter a figure between $5,000 and $41,100.)											
42												
43	Would you like to start receiving your CPP pension between the ages of 60 and 65?											**Y**
44	(It will be reduced by 6% for each year before age 65.)											
45												
46	If so, at what age would you like to start receiving your CPP pension?											**63**
47	(Enter an age between 60 and 64.)											
48												
49	**OTHER INCOME**											
50	How much money (before tax) from other sources in today's dollars do you expect each year after you retire?											**$1,000**
51	(For example, pension, self-employment, rental, investments outside RRSP.)											
52												
53	At what age do you expect this income from other sources to stop?											**70**
54												
55	**SPENDING**											
56	What is your current total income before taxes?											**$35,000**
57	(i.e., salary or net income from self-employment)											
58												
59	What percentage of your income before tax in today's dollars do you think you will need after you retire?											**50.00%**
60	(Note: The rule of thumb says about 70%, but depending on your situation it could be much lower --											
61	perhaps 40%.)											
62												
63	**LONGEVITY**											
64	Until what age do you think you will live? (Must be age 70 or older.)											**85**
65	(Note: If you have a spouse who you think will live longer than you, enter the age you would have been											
66	at the time of **his or her** death.)											

Notice that the questions are divided into categories as follows:

- General
- RRSP/RRIF
- Old Age Security
- Canada Pension Plan
- Other Income
- Spending
- Longevity

Let's go through Joe's answers to the questions in each category.

General

Joe has entered the current date of October 18, 2005, his name, and his birth date of January 2, 1955. He is therefore 50 years old at the time the spreadsheet was created.

RRSP/RRIF

Joe has entered his RRSP value of $95,000 and the fact that he plans to contribute $5,000 per year to it until he retires at age 65. Furthermore, he expects his RRSP investments to grow at an annual rate of 5 percent per year until he retires and 4 percent per year after he retires, since he will be switching to more conservative investments. He has also estimated inflation will average 2 percent per year for the rest of his life.

Old Age Security (OAS)

Anyone who has lived in Canada for 40 years or more between the age of 18 and his or her 65th birthday is eligible to receive the maximum OAS pension, starting at age 65. (As of the fourth quarter of 2005, that amount is $5,724 per year). Anyone who has lived in Canada for less than 40 years and more than 18 years will receive a pro-rated amount.

Joe will not meet the 40-year residency requirement, so he will not be eligible for the maximum OAS. He therefore has entered "N" for "No" in cell L29. (Notice that cell L29 is a pull-down menu. You simply click on the arrow on the right side of the cell, and highlight either "Y" or "N.") Since he will have lived in Canada for only 30 years since he turned 18, he has entered "30" in cell L32. As we'll see, the spreadsheet will estimate the pro-rated amount of OAS he is likely to receive upon retirement.

Canada Pension Plan (CPP)

The amount of Canada Pension Plan payments you receive after you retire will depend on how much you paid into the plan during your working life. If from age 18 to age 65 your earnings exceeded the Maximum Pensionable Earnings (MPE) amount as set by the government ($41,100 in 2005), you will receive the maximum payment per year ($9,945 in 2005) from the plan.

Joe has answered "N" to the question in L36 because he is not eligible to receive the maximum CPP pension. His annual earnings have averaged only $30,000 per year so he has entered "30,000" in cell L40. (Note that you can only enter an amount between $5,000 and $41,100 in that cell. This restriction reflects the basic exemption of $3,500 — and anything between that and $5,000 will be insignificant — and the MPE of $41,100.) The spreadsheet will automatically estimate the amount of CPP Joe is likely to receive.

You can make a request to the Federal Government to start receiving your CPP payments as early as age 60, but there is a catch. For every month before your 65th birthday, the CPP amount will be reduced by 0.5 percent. For every year you receive CPP before your 65th birthday, that's a reduction of 6 percent. Joe wants to start receiving his CPP at age 63, so he enters "Y" for Yes in cell L43 (another pull-down menu) and "63" in L46. If Joe chose not to start receiving his pension early, he would have left this cell blank.

Other income

Enter the details of any other income you will receive after you retire in this section. This income could include any company pension, self-employment income, rental income, and income from investments outside your RRSP. Note that the program asks for these amounts in today's dollars, not future dollars. This is because the program is designed to factor in inflation to project amounts to future dollars.

Joe is a handyman and figures he will earn about $1,000 per year from this work from age 65 to age 70. He has entered "1,000" in cell L50 and "70" in cell L53.

Spending

You must think carefully about how much money you will realistically need to support the lifestyle you want to have in retirement.

There is a rough rule of thumb that says that the average person will need approximately 70 percent of his or her pre-retirement earnings post-retirement in order to maintain his or her pre-retirement standard of living. This may or may not be the case for you. If you get your spending under control early in life, raise independent kids, and retire debt free and mortgage free, you could be fine with less than 40 percent of what you make now.

The amount of money you'll need after you stop working is a vital piece of information in your overall financial puzzle. It's really too important to leave up to some rule of thumb or estimate. That's why I encourage you to spend time on Step 4: Detailed Personal Financial Tracking.

Tracking your spending is the only way to determine what your expenses are likely to be in retirement. The added bonus is that it also gets you focused on where your money is going right now. That's why I call it the Ultimate Weapon in the fight to control your finances. It has the power to pinpoint your money drains — which means you can plug those drains and possibly save thousands of otherwise wasted dollars. It can also give you a clearer picture of how much you'll be spending in those years when you no longer earn a salary.

Since Joe doesn't track his spending and he makes $35,000 per year now, he estimates he'll need only 50 percent of that after he retires because he plans to be debt free. He enters "35,000" in cell L56 and "50" in cell L59.

Longevity

Joe figures he will live until age 85, so he enters "85" into cell L64.

You may notice when you fill in this spreadsheet with your own numbers that there is a note under this section about entering the age you would have been at the time of your spouse's death if you think he or she will live longer than you. Doing this allows the spreadsheet to delay the calculation of tax on the remaining RRIF balance until his or her death since the value can transfer tax free to your spouse upon your death.

EXCEL TIP

To limit the input for a cell to a certain range and to create an input message to help users enter valid data as well as error messages for ineligible data, select "Data" from the top menu, then select "Validation..."

The Results Tab

Figure 2-3 shows the Results tab. Here's where the details of Joe's situation come together so that he can see what his retirement income is likely to be.

The beauty of this program is that if things don't look good, Joe can go back to his answers and change them. (However, he'll also have to change his circumstances to match!) In other words, he'll be able to see immediately how any changes he makes now can help him secure or optimize his financial future.

The page layout is designed to print this tab in "landscape" so that the whole spreadsheet is easy to read.

The Results tab is divided into three sections: Input Summary, Results, and Detailed Results of Your Retirement Years. Let's look at each.

Input summary

The summary from lines 4 to 18 is simply a repeat of the information that Joe entered on the Questions tab. If he prints out the Results tab, he'll know exactly what the inputs were. This is important because if you have various scenarios printed out, you need to be able to see at a glance what the different input variables are for each set of results.

FIGURE 2-3 (1)

Retirement Optimizer Results for: Joe Fifty

INPUT SUMMARY

Date this analysis was prepared:	10/18/2005
The age you will be this month is:	50
Value of your RRSP on most recent statement:	$95,000
Annual RRSP contributions you plan to make from now until retirement:	$5,000
Age you plan to retire and stop making RRSP payments:	65
Annual rate at which you expect your RRSP to grow until you retire:	5.00%
Annual rate at which you expect your RRSP or RRIF to grow after you retire:	4.00%
Average annual inflation rate for the remainder of your life:	2.00%
Are you eligible for the maximum Old Age Security (OAS) pension at age 65?	No
Are you eligible for the maximum Canada Pension Plan (CPP) pension at age 65?	No
Amount of money from other sources (before tax) in today's dollars you expect each year after you retire:	$1,000
Age at which you expect this income from other sources to stop:	70
Your current total income before taxes is:	$35,000
Percentage of income before tax in today's dollars you think you will need after you retire:	50.00%
Age you think you (or your spouse) will live until:	85

RESULTS

At retirement your RRSP will be worth:	$305,391
The total amount of RRIF income will be forced to withdraw that you won't need:	$136,255
The total OAS pension amount per year (in future dollars) you will receive starting at age 65 is:	$5,778
The total CPP retirement pension amount per year (in future dollars) you could receive starting at age 65 is:	$9,770
Age you chose to start receiving your CPP retirement pension:	63
You have chosen to receive your CPP retirement pension early. The amount per year is:	$8,597
The value of your RRIF that will be taxed on your death (or your spouse's death if he/she lives longer):	$162,648
The approximate amount of income tax that will be lost on the RRIF upon death:	$69,563

DETAILED RESULTS OF YOUR RETIREMENT YEARS

RRSP YEARS

Age During Year**	RRSP Value Beginning of Year	RRSP Withdrawals	Increase in RRSP Value During Year	RRSP Value End of Year	OAS Payments*	CPP Payments*	Other Income*	Total Income	OAS Clawback*	Total Income	Required Income*	RRSP on Death
55	0	0	0	0	0		0	0	0	0		0
56	0	0	0	0	0		0	0	0	0		0
57	0	0	0	0	0		0	0	0	0		0
58	0	0	0	0	0		0	0	0	0		0
59	0	0	0	0	0		0	0	0	0		0
60	0	0	0	0	0	0	0	0	0	0		0
61	0	0	0	0	0	0	0	0	0	0		0
62	0	0	0	0	0	0	0	0	0	0		0
63	0	0	0	0	0	8,597	0	8,597	8,597	8,597		0
64	0	0	0	0	0	8,769	0	8,769	8,769	8,769		0
65	305,391	7,484	11,916	309,823	5,778	8,945	1,346	23,553	23,553	23,553	23,553	0
66	309,823	7,634	12,088	314,277	5,893	9,124	1,373	24,024	24,024	24,024	24,024	0
67	314,277	7,787	12,260	318,750	6,011	9,306	1,400	24,504	24,504	24,504	24,504	0
68	318,750	7,942	12,432	323,240	6,131	9,492	1,428	24,994	24,994	24,994	24,994	0
69	323,240	8,101	12,606	327,744	6,254	9,682	1,457	25,494	25,494	25,494	25,494	0

FIGURE 2-3 (2)

	A	B	C	D	E	F	G	H	I	J	K	L	M	N	O
55	RRIF YEARS														
	Age During Year**	RRIF Value Beginning of Year	Minimum RRIF Withdrawals	Additional RRIF Withdrawal to meet Required Income	Increase in RRIF Value During Year	RRIF Value End of Year	OAS Payments*	CPP Payments*	Other Income*	Total Income Before Add. RRIF	Total Income After Add. RRIF	OAS Clawback*	Total Income	Required Income*	Excess Income
61	70	327,744	15,607	0	12,485	324,623	6,379	9,876	1,486	33,348	33,348	0	33,348	26,004	7,344
62	71	324,623	16,231	0	12,336	320,727	6,507	10,073	0	32,811	32,811	0	32,811	26,524	6,287
63	72	320,727	23,670	0	11,882	308,940	6,637	10,275	0	40,581	40,581	0	40,581	27,055	13,527
64	73	308,940	23,109	0	11,433	297,264	6,770	10,480	0	40,359	40,359	0	40,359	27,596	12,763
65	74	297,264	22,562	0	10,988	285,690	6,905	10,690	0	40,157	40,157	0	40,157	28,148	12,010
66	75	285,690	22,027	0	10,547	274,210	7,043	10,904	0	39,973	39,973	0	39,973	28,711	11,263
67	76	274,210	21,525	0	10,107	262,792	7,184	11,122	0	39,831	39,831	0	39,831	29,285	10,546
68	77	262,792	20,997	0	9,672	251,467	7,328	11,344	0	39,669	39,669	0	39,669	29,871	9,798
69	78	251,467	20,495	0	9,239	240,211	7,474	11,571	0	39,540	39,540	0	39,540	30,468	9,072
70	79	240,211	20,010	0	8,808	229,009	7,624	11,802	0	39,436	39,436	0	39,436	31,077	8,358
71	80	229,009	19,534	0	8,379	217,854	7,776	12,039	0	39,349	39,349	0	39,349	31,699	7,650
72	81	217,854	19,062	0	7,952	206,743	7,932	12,279	0	39,273	39,273	0	39,273	32,333	6,940
73	82	206,743	18,586	0	7,526	195,683	8,090	12,525	0	39,201	39,201	0	39,201	32,979	6,222
74	83	195,683	18,140	0	7,102	184,645	8,252	12,775	0	39,167	39,167	0	39,167	33,639	5,528
75	84	184,645	17,689	0	6,678	173,635	8,417	13,031	0	39,137	39,137	0	39,137	34,312	4,825
76	85	173,635	17,242	0	6,256	162,648	8,586	13,291	0	39,119	39,119	0	39,119	34,998	4,121
77	86	0	0	0	0	0	0	0	0	0	0	0	0	0	0
78	87	0	0	0	0	0	0	0	0	0	0	0	0	0	0
79	88	0	0	0	0	0	0	0	0	0	0	0	0	0	0
80	89	0	0	0	0	0	0	0	0	0	0	0	0	0	0
81	90	0	0	0	0	0	0	0	0	0	0	0	0	0	0
82	91	0	0	0	0	0	0	0	0	0	0	0	0	0	0
83	92	0	0	0	0	0	0	0	0	0	0	0	0	0	0
84	93	0	0	0	0	0	0	0	0	0	0	0	0	0	0
85	94	0	0	0	0	0	0	0	0	0	0	0	0	0	0
86	95	0	0	0	0	0	0	0	0	0	0	0	0	0	0
87															
88													TOTALS		136,255

* Amounts adjusted for inflation

** You must convert your RRSP to a RRIF in the year you turn 69. The next year you must make your first RRIF withdrawal before December 31st. During this next year you are 69 at the beginning of the year and you turn 70 during the year.

EXCEL TIP

You can bring the contents of a cell from another tab to the cell you are currently in by entering the "equals" sign ("=") in the current cell, and then going to the other tab and clicking on the cell you want the contents brought from or enter the formula as follows:

=Questions!L6

This will bring the contents of cell L6 on the Questions tab and put it in the cell where you have entered the formula.

Results

Lines 21 to 29 show the amounts Joe can expect to receive in retirement, based on his specific answers to the questions in the Questions tab. These lines also show other key information such as the value of his RRSP at retirement, the excess he will likely have but not need, and the amount lost to taxes upon death.

Those key figures for Joe are —

- The value of his RRSP at retirement ($305,391)

- The total amount of RRIF income he will be forced to withdraw that he won't need ($136,255)

- The total OAS pension amount per year he will receive starting at age 65 in future dollars ($5,778)

- The total CPP pension amount he will receive per year in future dollars if he starts at age 65 ($9,770)

- If he elects to receive CPP early, the age he elected to start and the amount per year he will get (63, $8,597)

- The total amount of OAS pension that will be clawed back over the years, if any (none for Joe so this line (27) shows as blank)

- The value of his RRIF that will be taxed upon his death, or his spouse's death, should she live longer ($162,648)

- The approximate amount of income tax that will be lost on the RRIF upon death ($69,563)

Detailed results of your retirement years

RRSP years

The Detailed Results of Your Retirement Years is a table that shows year by year what your income from all sources will be from retirement until death from as early as age 55 to as late as age 95. Each column is labelled across the top with the name of the income source or the investment whose value is shown. The rows are clearly labelled down the left side with an age for each row, going year by year. As you scan horizontally across each row, you can see how much income can be expected from each source at any age, as well as the value of each investment. Let's have a look at Joe's results.

The RRSP value at the beginning of the year Joe retires at age 65 is $305,391 (cell B49). His required income for the year ($23,553) is shown in cell M49. That figure is the future value of his current required income of $17,500 (50 percent of his $35,000 salary) projected 15 years into the future at a 2 percent increase per year.

The amount in cell C49 is a calculated figure that makes the total income including OAS, CPP, other income, and the RRSP withdrawal equal to the required income. This is the amount Joe would have to withdraw from his RRSP to bring his income from all sources up to the required amount. Joe therefore receives $5,778 from OAS, $8,945 from CPP,

$1,346 from other income, and $7,484 from his RRSP. The total is the required $23,553.

The increase in RRSP value during the year shown in cell D49 ($11,916) is the beginning value of $305,391 less the withdrawal of $7,484 times the rate of return he expects after retirement (4 percent). In other words ($305,391 − $7,484) x 0.04 = $11,916. Note that we are assuming the RRSP withdrawal is being made at the beginning of the year. In most cases, RRSP (and later RRIF) withdrawals will be made monthly. That would result in even higher RRSP/RRIF values than the spreadsheet shows because the money is being left in longer to grow before being taken out.

The closing RRSP value is the value at the beginning of the year less the withdrawal plus the increase. For Joe, the equation is $305,391 − $7,484 + $11,916 = $309,823 (cell E49).

Note that in Joe's case, there is no OAS clawback because his income never exceeds the limit of $60,806, which is where the clawback begins (in 2005). This limit is indexed to inflation, like the OAS payments themselves, so in 15 years, the limit will actually be $81,837 — the future value of $60,806 at 2 percent inflation per year for 15 years. (The OAS and CPP limits are shown on the TaxInfo tab at lines 61 to 71, reproduced here on page 31.)

RRIF years

You cannot continue making RRSP contributions past age 69. In fact, you must convert your RRSP to a RRIF (Registered Retirement Income Fund) or annuity by the end of the year you turn 69, and the next year you must make your first RRIF withdrawal before December 31.

So the RRSP years end at age 69, and the RRIF years start the year you turn 70. On the spreadsheet, the results for the RRIF years are shown underneath the RRSP years.

RRIF withdrawals are mandatory, and the government has set minimum RRIF withdrawal percentages from age 70. They are shown on the TaxInfo tab at lines 25 to 58 (see page 31).

The Additional RRIF Withdrawal to Meet Required Income (Column D) only kicks in if you need to take more out of your RRIF to meet your required income needs. In Joe's case, the year he turns 70, the total income (RRIF, OAS, CPP, and other income) comes to $33,348, whereas his required income is only $26,004. Even without any excess RRIF withdrawal, he has excess income of the difference — $7,344.

As we discussed earlier, if Joe had optimized his RRSP, it would have been smaller and this would therefore not have happened. He could have invested the extra money he put into his RRSP into something outside his RRSP — equity investments or even a vacation property, for example — and improved his tax and financial situation in the process.

There are a few things to note for Joe's RRIF years:

• Other income stops at age 70

• There will always be a minimum RRIF withdrawal as long as he lives

• OAS and CPP pension payments also continue until death

• The excess income he will be forced to withdraw and pay tax on over the course of his RRIF years totals $136,255 (cell O88)

• When he dies at age 85, his RRIF will still be worth $162,648 (cell F76)

As we've discussed, Joe can do better. First of all, he should play with all his input numbers, including his retirement age, RRSP/RRIF rates of return, longevity, and his retirement date. He needs to ensure that he doesn't run out of RRSP money even if, for example, he lives longer or his investments don't do as well as he hoped. Only then should he consider reducing his RRSP contributions to reduce the value of his RRSP. That's what optimizing is all about: building an RRSP that is ample size while eliminating all debt and investing any excess money in areas outside your RRSP.

Remember that all these variables are constantly changing. It's important to keep your Retirement Optimizer up to date year after year. It's easy to do and vital to your future financial well-being.

Try It with Your Own Figures

Just as you did with the Net Worth Calculator, try running the Retirement Optimizer with your own numbers. Answer all the questions on the Questions tab with your own information by inputting it over the sample data. You may be surprised by what you discover. Remember that you can adjust the data to see what a few changes can do for your situation.

What If I Run Out of Money?

If you enter all your own personal information, you might discover that you'll run out of money before you die. While that may be depressing, at least you've figured it out in time to take action!

If consulted in a situation like this, a financial planner (particularly one motivated by self-interest) is likely to recommend what to him or her is the obvious solution: you need to give him/her more RRSP money!

Well, that is one answer. But there are at least several others. Consider the following:

- **Reduce your spending requirements:** Perhaps you figure you'll need 60 percent of your pre-retirement earnings to maintain your standard of living once you stop working. But as I often say, if you have managed to pay off all debt, including the house mortgage, and have raised independent kids who are now supporting themselves, you may be fine with as little as 40 percent of your current earnings.

    You could also spend time on one of the biggest cash-drainers of all: your car. Head to Step 5 to find out how to save thousands of dollars with your car decisions. Also always remember to focus on your debt levels. Retiring in debt will cause you to need significantly more money after you retire to continue making the payments, as we'll see in the next chapter.

- **Reduce your taxes:** There is one major step you can take to minimize your family taxes. First and foremost for most Canadians is the Spousal RRSP. This allows spouses to even up RRSP values between the two of them, and that should be your objective, too, by the time you retire. You don't want one of you to have a huge RRSP that will cause the problems we have just seen, such as excess RRIF withdrawals and OAS clawbacks. If both spouses have similar-size RRSPs, the withdrawal income will be split, which results in a lesser amount of income being reported on two tax returns rather than a large amount on one — which results in a lower total tax bill. A spousal RRSP allows you to split your income: the contributor gets the tax deduction but his/her spouse can withdraw the RRSP/RRIF money later (subject to some rules regarding early withdrawals, etc.).

  Bear in mind that reducing taxes DOES NOT mean going out and grabbing the latest tax shelter. That is one of the worst things you could do. Why? Because you may lose ALL your money. Can you afford that risk?

- **Delay your retirement:** It's often amazing what even one year's delay will do. That's because in the last years of your working life, your RRSP is at its largest. Every additional year you leave this large nest egg to grow will give you the biggest return for your money. Often this strategy alone can turn a shortfall of money into a surplus.

- **Get better returns on your investments:** Do you know what the average rate of return is on your RRSP since you started making contributions? Most people don't, and in most cases the rate of return is very low. I have seen many instances where the return is, in fact, negative. How about focusing on getting your money to work harder for you instead of pouring more money in? Try it yourself using the Retirement Optimizer. Increasing your projected return by even just 1 percent a year can make a huge difference in your ability to fund your retirement. We'll address this in detail in the next section.

As you can see, there are many factors that determine whether or not you will have enough money in your own twilight years. None of them is set in stone. No matter what age you are, you can take control by using the Retirement Optimizer. The spreadsheet will do the calculations for you — but, of course, you'll have to do the heavy lifting to make the necessary changes happen. The starting point is here: you can either take control of your own destiny or leave it in the hands of others.

The Charts Tab

If you like to see a graphic representation of your retirement asset balance and your income, click on the Charts tab (see Figure 2-4). This repeats the input information, just as the Results tab does, and shows you a graph of your RRSP/RRIF value at the end of each of your RRPS/RRIF years.

It also has a second graph of your retirement income broken down by component (CPP, OAS, other income, minimum RRIF, and additional RRIF).

The Assumptions Tab

This tab lists the basic assumptions that have gone into building the Retirement Optimizer (see Figure 2-5).

FIGURE 2-4

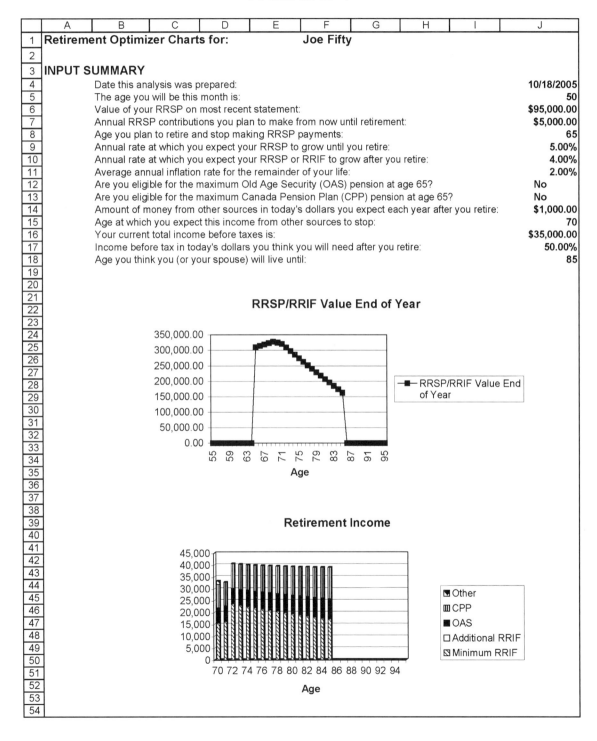

	A	B	C	D	E	F	G	H	I	J
1	**Retirement Optimizer Charts for:**					**Joe Fifty**				
2										
3	**INPUT SUMMARY**									
4		Date this analysis was prepared:								**10/18/2005**
5		The age you will be this month is:								**50**
6		Value of your RRSP on most recent statement:								**$95,000.00**
7		Annual RRSP contributions you plan to make from now until retirement:								**$5,000.00**
8		Age you plan to retire and stop making RRSP payments:								**65**
9		Annual rate at which you expect your RRSP to grow until you retire:								**5.00%**
10		Annual rate at which you expect your RRSP or RRIF to grow after you retire:								**4.00%**
11		Average annual inflation rate for the remainder of your life:								**2.00%**
12		Are you eligible for the maximum Old Age Security (OAS) pension at age 65?								**No**
13		Are you eligible for the maximum Canada Pension Plan (CPP) pension at age 65?								**No**
14		Amount of money from other sources in today's dollars you expect each year after you retire:								**$1,000.00**
15		Age at which you expect this income from other sources to stop:								**70**
16		Your current total income before taxes is:								**$35,000.00**
17		Income before tax in today's dollars you think you will need after you retire:								**50.00%**
18		Age you think you (or your spouse) will live until:								**85**

FIGURE 2-5

	A	B	C	D	E	F	G	H	I
1	**Retirement Optimizer Assumptions**								
2									
3	1. RRSP and RRIF withdrawals take place on January 1st of each year.								
4									
5	2. Personal taxes are calculated at 2005 Ontario rates.								
6									
7	3. OAS, CPP, and other income increase each year at the inflation rate you input on the Questions tab.								

The TaxInfo Tab

The TaxInfo tab for Joe Fifty is shown in Figure 2-6. It has detailed tax rates for Ontario for 2005. The only reason this is here is to calculate the estimated personal income tax that would be payable on the remaining RRIF balance on the death of the second spouse. If you are in another province or territory, you'll need to update this chart. (Check the updates page of Self-Counsel Press's website at www.self-counsel.com for additional worksheets with tax information specific to your province.) That will give you a more accurate figure, but probably not a significantly different one.

A Word about Keeping Current

You can now keep the Retirement Optimizer up to date because I have unprotected the entire spreadsheet. You'll need to go to the TaxInfo tab to update the following:

Personal income tax rates by province: Cells A9 to D19

Minimum RRIF withdrawal percentages: Cells A33 to B58

OAS **details:** Cells E63 to E66 (includes maximum payout amount per year, taxable income where clawback begins, rate of clawback, and taxable income where all OAS is clawed back).

CPP **maximum benefit payable per year:** Cell E71

FIGURE 2-6

	A	B	C	D	E	F	G	H	I	J	K	L	M
1	**Tax Information Page**												
2													
3	Combined 2005 Federal and Ontario Personal Income Tax Rates												
4													
5					Marginal Rate On					Reg			
6	Lower	Upper	Basic	Rate on	Dividend	Capital		Total	Total	Net Income	Reg	RRIF	RRIF
7	limit	Limit	Tax	Excess	Income	Gains		Tax Inc	Tax	Death Year	Tax	Tax Inc	Tax
8													
9	0.00	8,148.00	0.00	0.00%	0.00%	0.00%		$201,767.21		$39,118.91		$162,648.30	
10	8,149.00	11,336.00	0.00	16.00%	3.33%	8.00%							
11	11,337.00	14,477.00	510.00	28.10%	5.63%	14.05%							
12	14,478.00	34,010.00	1,393.00	22.05%	4.48%	11.03%							
13	34,011.00	35,595.00	5,700.00	25.15%	8.36%	12.58%							
14	35,596.00	59,882.00	6,098.00	31.15%	15.86%	15.58%					$7,195.39		
15	59,883.00	68,020.00	13,664.00	32.98%	16.86%	16.49%							
16	68,021.00	70,559.00	16,348.00	35.39%	19.88%	17.70%							
17	70,560.00	71,190.00	17,246.00	39.41%	22.59%	19.70%							
18	71,191.00	115,739.00	17,495.00	43.41%	27.59%	21.70%							
19	115,740.00		36,833.00	46.41%	31.34%	23.20%			$76,758.23				
20													
21									$76,758.23		$7,195.39		$69,562.84
22	Note: Tax rates include provincial surtaxes and reflect budget proposals and news releases to February 23, 2005												
23													
24													
25	**RRIF Minimum Payments from Age 69**												
26													
27													
28	Age of												
29	Annuitant												
30	or spouse	RRIF											
31	or common	Withdrawal											
32	law partner	Rate											
33	69	0.0476											
34	70	0.0500											
35	71	0.0738											
36	72	0.0748											
37	73	0.0759											
38	74	0.0771											
39	75	0.0785											
40	76	0.0799											
41	77	0.0815											
42	78	0.0833											
43	79	0.0853											
44	80	0.0875											
45	81	0.0899											
46	82	0.0927											
47	83	0.0958											
48	84	0.0993											
49	85	0.1033											
50	86	0.1079											
51	87	0.1133											
52	88	0.1196											
53	89	0.1271											
54	90	0.1362											
55	91	0.1473											
56	92	0.1612											
57	93	0.1792											
58	94 or older	0.2000											
59													
60													
61	**OAS Details**				2005	2004	2003						
62													
63	Maximum OAS amount per year:				5,724	5,556	5,440						
64	Taxable income where clawback begins:				60,806	59,790	57,879						
65	Reduction per dollar earned:				0.15	0.15	0.15						
66	Taxable income where all OAS clawed back:				98,793	96,830	94,146						
67													
68													
69	**CPP Details**				2005	2004							
70													
71	Maximum benefit payable per year:				9,945	9,768							

Step 3

THE GREAT DEBATE: RRSP VERSUS PAYING OFF DEBT

When RRSP season rolls around each February, the papers are filled with articles about the merits of putting money into RRSPs versus using that money to pay down the mortgage. The common conclusion is that you should maximize your RRSP contribution and use the tax refund you'll get from doing so to pay down the mortgage. This plan sounds good, but in reality it is just a trick to get you to part with more of your hard-earned money.

Consider who is sending out this message. It's all the usual suspects: banks, brokerage firms, mutual fund companies, and the people that make a living by pushing their products. Why do they want you to fall for this message? Because for every dollar you put in, they get a percentage. It's a guaranteed annuity for them, regardless of what happens to your investments along the way.

Retiring with a huge nest egg seems desirable, but as we discussed in Step 2, that same nest egg can lead to you paying excessive tax during your retirement — not to mention that you may never get to spend a substantial amount of that cash you're busily socking away now. Paying off your mortgage more quickly than required, however, could leave you debt free sooner than you'd imagined. But how can you decide which choice is right for you?

You simply cannot determine whether it's better for you to max out your RRSP contribution or use that money to pay down your mortgage without first determining one vital statistic: the size your RRSP will need to be at retirement.

That's why I put the chapter on optimizing your retirement before this one. You must go through the exercise of determining what your income and spending will be after you retire. Only then can you determine how big your own RRSP will need to be. Once you have that information, you can address whether you'll need to put more money into your RRSP in order to meet your retirement goals or use that money to pay down the mortgage.

The next factor to consider is how well your RRSP has done in the past and how well it might do in the future. Obviously, this can have a huge effect on how large your RRSP will grow and how long it will last after you retire. If you do nothing else on your finances, spend time focusing on this issue. It's one of the easiest ways to make major gains in your net worth because it doesn't require you to work more hours or cut back on your lifestyle. All it takes is a little of your time right now.

How Well Is Your RRSP Doing?

Does it make sense to continue to put money into an RRSP that is performing poorly? How can you possibly decide if paying off debt would be better than maxing out your RRSP contribution if you don't know what rate of return you have been getting on your RRSP and what it's likely to be in the future? The decision is a lot easier if you know you've been earning only 2 percent a year and you have a mortgage at 6 percent. It's necessary to take the time to figure out what your RRSP personal rate of return has been. It could mean the difference between a comfortable retirement and a miserable one.

Two Ways to Build an RRSP

I remember years ago having a conversation with my broker. At that stage in my life, I was more interested in having fun than worrying about retirement, but I was still concerned with the question of how big my RRSP would have to be for me to retire comfortably. The problem was that the investments in my RRSP had not been doing well.

When I confronted my broker with this situation, he said the solution was for me to put more money into my RRSP.

I remember feeling conned. Here was a big brokerage firm ignoring my concerns about lousy investment returns and telling me the way to solve my problem was to give them more money. On that day I got angry and resolved to take better control of my family's investments. First, I created the Personal Rate of Return Calculator we will discuss next. It confirmed my suspicions about how poorly my investments were performing. Then I found myself a new adviser. (We'll talk more about advisers later.)

There are two key strategies involved in building an RRSP. One requires sacrifice, and the other takes very little effort. Here they are:

1. Maximize the amount of money invested

2. Maximize the rate of return earned

Let's face it: Strategy 1 means finding thousands of dollars every year for an RRSP contribution, and that can be very difficult. It means working hard and cutting back on other spending to come up with the cash.

But what about Strategy 2? Are you doing all you can to make sure the money already in your RRSP is growing at an adequate rate? I don't know about you, but I spend time every month going over our family RRSP and investment statements focused on one thing: how well the investments are doing. I cringe every time I hear of people who don't open the monthly statements from their brokers because they are "afraid to look." Some people even pretend to be proud of this. What are they thinking? Do they care about their family's future?

If you ignore your investments' performance, you'll have to work a lot harder to make up for lousy investment returns. But RRSP statements can be incredibly complicated, and they almost never show your actual rate of return. That's why I created the Personal Rate of Return Calculator (PRR).

The Personal Rate of Return Calculator

The Personal Rate of Return Calculator is easy to use. It's a one-page spreadsheet. The hardest part about using it is gathering the information you'll need. That is a listing of the amounts and dates you made contributions to your RRSP. You'll need to go back to the day you started your account. One way to get this information is to ask the investment adviser who handles your RRSP for it. He or she will have the information, and you have the right to demand it. It may take a while to get it from him or her, but it will be worth the wait.

Alternatively, you can go through your old tax returns and look for the slips you filed with your returns. If you don't know the exact day you made the contribution, use the end of the month in which it was made.

The program computes the effective annual rate, which takes into account the compounding period — in this case, a year. All you need to know is the dollar amount and dates you originally invested and the total current market value of all the related portfolios. The cells in which you need to input information are shown in bold typeface in columns B and C. All other cells are calculated by the program.

You should be aware of a couple of points. First, the program assumes any dividends from stocks and distributions from mutual funds are reinvested in the RRSP. This is usually the case with RRSPs. Second, the program does not account for withdrawals from the RRSP because this results in many calculation complexities. If you withdraw money from your RRSP, calculate your rate of return to the withdrawal date and then start future personal rate of return calculations from that withdrawal date.

To use the Personal Rate of Return Calculator, you will need to have the "Solver" add-in to your Microsoft Excel program. Unfortunately, it usually doesn't come pre-installed. If you select "Tools" and see "Solver..." as a choice, you're ready to go. If not, here's how to install it:

- From the "Tools" menu, select "Add-Ins..."

- In the "Add-Ins available" box, select "Solver Add-In."

- A box will come up saying, "Microsoft Excel can't run this add-in. This feature is not currently installed. Would you like to install it now?" Click "Yes."

- Excel may say that the feature you are trying to use is on a CD-ROM that is not available. Insert the CD that has Excel on it, and it will search for the needed file.

- Click "OK" and the solver should be installed.

To help you understand how to use the Personal Rate of Return Calculator spreadsheet, I have created a hypothetical case study. Have a look at Figure 3-1. Alternatively, open the Personal Rate of Return Calculator on your computer and go to the Input & Results tab. You'll see that I have input sample data into Columns B and C. When you come to do your own calculations, just input your own information over the sample data.

On the Input & Results tab, I have entered the date to which calculations are done in cell E6. (That's the date that you have the current market value of all investments. In the case on the spreadsheet, I have entered "12/31/2005." For you, it could be "31/12/2005," depending on how your dates are displayed.)

FIGURE 3-1

	A	B	C	D	E
1	THE PERSONAL RATE OF RETURN CALCULATOR				
2	Version 91105				
3					
4					
5					
6	ENTER DATE TO WHICH CALCULATIONS DONE IN CELL E6				12/31/2005
7					
8		Date	Amount	# of days	Value
9		contributed	contributed	to calculation	at calculation
10				date	date
11					
12	Enter date and amount in columns B & C		0.00	38717	0.00
13	Cells in columns D & E are calculated	2/28/1995	2,500.00	3959	1,813.16
14		1/31/1996	3,500.00	3622	2,608.80
15		2/28/1997	4,000.00	3228	3,078.33
16		2/28/1998	4,200.00	2863	3,329.40
17		6/30/1998	3,500.00	2741	2,802.10
18		2/29/2000	5,000.00	2132	4,205.76
19		1/31/1999	4,800.00	2526	3,910.51
20		2/28/2004	6,000.00	672	5,681.62
21		2/28/2003	5,500.00	1037	5,056.17
22		1/31/2001	4,800.00	1795	4,149.45
23		1/15/2002	6,000.00	1446	5,335.79
24		3/1/2005	7,000.00	305	6,828.90
25					
26					
27	Total contributions		56,800.00		
28					
29	FINAL TOTAL MARKET VALUE (should agree with statement)				48,800.00
30					
31	GROWTH DOLLAR AMOUNT OVER CONTRIBUTIONS				-8,000.00
32					
33	AVERAGE ANNUAL INTERNAL RATE OF RETURN (calculated]				-2.92%

Enter each of your original investment amounts and corresponding dates in cells B12 to C24. If you need more lines, simply insert a line in Excel and copy the formulas from cells in Columns D and E in the line above. Note that the order the amounts are entered is not important since the formulas in Columns D and E are not affected by the line the entries are made on.

The program totals all the original contributions in cell C27. In this case, it's $56,800. It will also calculate the final total market value in cell E29, which won't agree to the actual total until after the next step.

Now the solver comes in:

- Select "Tools" and then "Solver..."

- In the "Set Target Cell:" box, enter E29 or simply click on that cell. (Excel will put a $ sign before the letter and the number. Don't worry about that.)

- After "Equal To:" select the "Value of:" button and enter the total current market value; "48,800" in this example.

- In the "By Changing Cells:" box, enter E33 (or just click on that cell).

- Click on the "Solve" button, and there's our answer: − 2.92%.

The program works backwards to solve for the rate of return that would bring your original investments up to the current market value.

You then have the option of keeping the solver solution or restoring the original values in the program. Keep the solver solution if you wish and just save the file under another name. This way you will keep the original program intact so you can start from scratch later.

That's all there is to it.

Combined Family Rate of Return

Now that you know what your personal rate of return is on your own RRSP, if you have a spouse or partner, do the same calculations for his/her RRSP. After that, simply cut and paste your details and his or hers into a new PRR calculator and see what the combined rate of return has been.

Armed with this data, you are now in a position to address the RRSP versus paying off debt question. In some cases, the choice is simple. If you have credit card debt at 20 percent interest and your RRSPs have been earning 2 percent a year, stop making RRSP payments and get rid of the credit card debt now. Remember that people who sell mutual funds for a living don't bring up a question like "RRSP or pay off the credit card at 20 percent?" That's because it's a no-brainer!

However, if your RRSP has been making a strong 6 percent a year, and you have a mortgage at only 4.5 percent and you have determined that you still need to grow your RRSP significantly, keep making those RRSP contributions and take care of the mortgage later.

The Transparency of Debt

Most of us have at least some debt. Debt is not all bad. Without it, very few of us would own a home or drive a car.

Debt is much easier to track than investments. Take your mortgage for example. You know exactly what interest rate you are paying at all times. It's the same thing with a credit card balance. If you pay off these debts, you know exactly what rate of return you are making on your money — it's the interest rate on the debt.

How can you make a rate of return by paying off debt? Easy — by saving the interest you would have paid if you'd had to keep carrying the debt. Pay off the debt, and that's less money in the form of interest flowing out of your pocket. That's just as good as more money flowing in from investments — better, in fact, because most interest on personal debt such as credit cards and mortgages (in most cases) is not tax deductible, whereas investment income (outside an RRSP and inside after withdrawal) is taxable.

Bottom line: Paying off non-deductible debt at 5 percent is better than an investment earning 5 percent, because part of the income is lost to tax.

But What about the Tax Refund I Get from My RRSP Contribution?

There is an economic benefit to the reduction in current taxes you get when you make an RRSP contribution, but there is also a cost. We saw that with Jim Bradley in Chapter 7 of *Smoke and Mirrors: Financial Myths That Will Ruin Your Retirement Dreams*. He maxed out his RRSP and ended up paying taxes on more than $311,000 of income he didn't need but was forced to withdraw because of the minimum RRIF withdrawal rules.

There is another key issue here: What are you doing with your refund? Many Canadians see it as some kind of windfall and end up spending it on a vacation or new toy. This is like "un-saving" for retirement: You're creating a situation in which you'll pay more taxes in the future so you can spend more than you earn right now.

We've seen that situation with the Retirement Optimizer. Upon retirement, every withdrawal you make from your RRSP will be taxable. That's the trade-off for getting a refund on those contributions. It sounds great now, but if you're not careful it could come back to haunt you later.

If you do make an RRSP contribution, at least use the refund to pay off whatever debt you may have.

A Compromise Solution

For many people, making a little compromise works best. Instead of pouring as much as possible into their RRSPs, they pay down debt with half the money and make an RRSP contribution with the other half.

They then use the tax refund to further pay down debt or invest outside their RRSPs in an area they feel confident they could get a good rate of return.

In the case of spouses, they may alternate each other's RRSP contribution each year. Again, it should go without saying that if you choose this strategy, you must carefully track your RRSP and make sure the money is being invested wisely.

Is My Investment Adviser/Firm Any Good?

If you want to make good returns on your RRSP, you'll need a good investment adviser. I strongly urge you to think about the qualities of the person(s) looking after your money. If your adviser is good and trustworthy, your life will be much easier for it. But if you get stuck with someone who is self-interested, unqualified, or simply a scam artist, you could lose everything. Ask yourself the following questions:

1. Does my adviser care about my debt?

Has your adviser ever asked you how much debt you have? If not, chances are he or she doesn't care.

Your adviser may have even tried to convince you to borrow to invest more. This could be disastrous and could leave you with a large amount of debt. You'd have to hope for good returns on your investments just so you could keep up your loan payments after you retire.

I've said it before and I will say it again: Your objective should be to retire debt free. Your adviser should be with you 100 percent on this. Bring it up the next time you meet with your adviser and find out if he or she wants to discuss it. If not, that should be a dead giveaway: your adviser is interested only in his or her own retirement, not yours.

I've even seen invitations for "information sessions" from brokerage firms with a bold assertion such as —

> *"Invitation only for those with investable assets, excluding real estate, of at least $500,000."*

Here is what they are really saying:

> *"We don't care about you if you can't make us a lot of money."*

2. Are the statements my adviser sends me easy to understand?

Go get your latest RRSP statement right now. Look for your personal annual rate of return for the year-to-date and for the last one-, two-, three-, five-, and ten-year periods. Can you see it?

Chances are, you'll see lots of numbers — current market value, market value on the last statement date, contributions for the current year, and perhaps book-value information — but you won't see anything related to your rate of return.

How are you supposed to know how well you are doing? You're paying your adviser all kinds of fees; why doesn't he or she tell you what you need to know? Surely it's not too complicated for him or her to determine your rate of return. That can't be the case: It took me only a few hours to create the Personal Rate of Return Calculator; and surely your adviser should be able to do something similar for you. Perhaps the excuse is that your adviser thinks it would be too hard for you to understand.

Excuse me? The real reason advisers don't talk about your personal rate of return is simple: YOUR ADVISER DOESN'T WANT YOU TO KNOW.

Why? Because if you knew you were making only a 1.2 percent return on your investments instead of the 8 percent you hoped to make, you'd probably make some changes, wouldn't you? That might even include taking your money somewhere else, and that would hit your adviser where it counts — in the big fat pocketbook.

3. Am I sticking with my adviser out of friendship or blind trust?

How did you find your financial adviser? For many people, it's the same way they found their doctor or dentist — through a personal contact. Maybe your adviser is your neighbour or a friend of a friend. Your adviser may even be a relative. But is he or she handling your money effectively? Is he or she qualified, educated, insured? Does he or she answer your questions in plain language and return your calls when you have concerns?

It's sad, but in a lot of cases, people stick with their advisers their whole lives, not because these advisers are good but because they are nice. That's costly and possibly a recipe for disaster. Good advisers are hard to find but are well worth the effort. Don't let yourself become a victim: If your adviser is no good, fire him or her and find someone who is. Your family's future is at stake.

If you are interested in finding out whether or not your adviser is any good, try sending him/her a formal memo raising all your concerns and see what the response is. Don't do this in a phone call. It's easy for them to brush you off or simply ignore your call.

I have drafted a memo for you to use as a template. You'll find it as an appendix at the back of this workbook. You'll note that it touches on many problems common to adviser-managed RRSPs. These are all addressed in *Smoke and Mirrors: Financial Myths That Will Ruin Your Retirement Dreams*. Not all of the issues may apply to your situation so customize it as you see fit.

How Big an RRSP Will I Need If I'm Not Debt Free at Retirement?

The temptation to max out your RRSP each year can be great. After all, by government regulation, you can contribute up to 18 percent of your income to your RRSP year by year. But this formula is based on the assumption that when combined with OAS and CPP pensions, you'll have approximately 70 percent of you pre-retirement income after you stop working. But if you concentrate instead on paying off debt — including your mortgage — as quickly as possible, you can live comfortably on considerably less.

However, if you put all your eggs in the RRSP basket and don't worry about paying off debt, you'll likely retire in debt. If you do, you'll still be making debt payments after you retire. Where's that money going to come from? Probably from your RRSP. Simply stated, your RRSP is going to have to be a lot bigger to finance those debt payments.

I have created a spreadsheet, the RRSP Value Projector for Mortgage at Retirement, to help illustrate this point. Look at Figure 3-2. Alternatively, open the spreadsheet on your computer.

In this example, a 45-year-old is considering buying a house, but won't be able to pay off the mortgage by the time he retires. He estimates that he'll still have $100,000 to pay

FIGURE 3-2

	A	B
1	**RRSP Value Projector for Mortgage at Retirement**	
2		
3	**Answer these questions:**	
4	How old are you now?	45
5		
6	At what age do you plan to retire?	65
7		
8	What will your mortage balance be at retirement?	$100,000
9		
10	How many years will there be left on your mortgage?	10
11	(after you retire)	
12		
13	What annual interest rate will your mortgage have?	5.00%
14		
15	What rate of return do you expect on your RRSP BEFORE retirement?	6.00%
16		
17	What rate of return do you expect on your RRSP AFTER retirement?	4.00%
18		
19	What will your marginal tax rate be after retirement?	40.00%
20		
21		
22	**Your Results:**	
23		
24	Your monthly mortgage payments are approximately:	**$1,056**
25		
26	The pre-tax monthly income you'll need from your RRSP to pay	
27	your mortgage will be:	**$1,760**
28		
29	Your RRSP will have to be this much bigger just to make your mortgage payments:	**$174,457**
30		
31	Number of years to retirement:	**20**
32		
33	Amount you will have to save per MONTH until retirement to reach the required RRSP value:	**$376**
34		
35	Amount you will have to save per YEAR until retirement to reach the required RRSP value:	**$4,512**

off and that the mortgage will have 10 years remaining when he does retire at age 65. This spreadsheet shows how much bigger his RRSP will need to be at retirement to pay for a $100,000 mortgage that still has 10 years to go.

In Column B, I have entered the answers to the questions in cells A4 to A19 about age (45), retirement age (65), mortgage balance at retirement ($100,000), years left on the mortgage at retirement (10), mortgage interest rate (5 percent), RRSP rate of return before (6 percent) and after retirement (4 percent), and marginal tax bracket (40 percent). (To find your marginal tax bracket, check your personal income tax return or ask your accountant.)

Now look at the results shown in cells B24 to B35. In this case, the RRSP would need to be $174,457 larger at retirement just to make all the mortgage payments of $1,056 per month. That's because at a 40 percent marginal tax bracket, the RRSP would have to pay out $1,760 per month before tax.

This person, who hasn't even bought the house yet, would have to save an extra $4,512 per year for the next 20 years to retirement and hope for the 6 percent annual RRSP rate of return in order to continue making the mortgage payments in retirement.

Simply retiring debt free eliminates a lot of the risks and anxieties of retirement: you get a guaranteed rate of return by paying off debt, as we discussed above; your income — and therefore your taxes — will be lower after you retire; and you'll have less risk of a costly OAS clawback. You'll also virtually eliminate the risk of losing your home.

That sounds like a solid plan to me.

Just for Fun

There are people out there trying to convince you that retiring "rich" can be easy. All you have to do is make a few changes such as skipping your cup of coffee every morning.

Let's not get into the emotional aspect of eliminating one of the pleasures in life. Instead, let's work through some numbers.

Look at Figure 3-3. It's the Coffee-skipping Way to Retirement Projector. The subject is 45 years old and wants to retire at 65. His daily coffee costs him $2.50 and he estimates that his "coffee savings" will earn a rate of return of 6 percent per year.

FIGURE 3-3

	A	B
1	**Coffee-skipping Way to Retirement Projector**	
2		
3	**Answer these questions:**	
4	How old are you now?	45
5		
6	At what age do you plan to retire?	65
7		
8	What annual rate of return do you expect on your invested "coffee savings"?	6.00%
9		
10	How much does your coffee cost?	$2.50
11		
12	**Your Results:**	
13		
14	Number of years to retirement:	**20**
15		
16	If you skip your coffee every day for that many years, you would have this much at retirement:	**$35,286**
17		
18		
19	**Notes:**	
20	1. Assumes you skip your coffee EVERY day, not just work days.	
21	2. Assumes the investments grow outside an RRSP but grow tax free.	

Even assuming that the invested savings grow tax-free and he skips his coffee 365 days a year, he ends up with only $35,286 in resulting savings at age 65. Hey, where's my million dollars?

Try it yourself by entering your own information into cells B4 to B10.

Step 4

DETAILED PERSONAL FINANCIAL TRACKING

O.K. We're agreed that eliminating coffee from your daily life is probably not going to solve all your financial problems, but what will?

How about focusing on your biggest expenses and gaining control of them?

It just makes sense that you'll get ahead further and faster if you can curb a large expense rather then a small one, and that brings you to your next problem: What are your largest expenses?

For most of us the big ones include housing costs (mortgage interest and property taxes or rent), automobile costs (more about them in Step 5), children's education, and income tax. Your list may be quite different from this, but you need to discover what your major costs are and how big they are before you can begin to control them.

How are you going to do that?

There is one good way — detailed personal financial tracking. It's so powerful that I call it the "Ultimate Weapon" in the battle to control your personal finances, and I devote a whole chapter to it in *Smoke and Mirrors: Financial Myths That Will Ruin Your Retirement Dreams.*

Money Drain Pain

The reason detailed tracking is so helpful is that it clearly shows you where the problems are, such as poor investment returns and wasted money such as interest on credit card debt. Let me try to convince you by using a spreadsheet I call Money Drain Pain.

This little spreadsheet is a reality check. It shows you how many hours of work you are wasting by ignoring your personal finances.

Have a look at Figure 4-1, or open the Money Drain Pain spreadsheet on your computer. In this example, I have assumed that this person is wasting $1,000 a year by ignoring his or her finances.

In many cases, this is not an unreasonable amount of money to save in a year. Just eliminate a few late credit card payments by paying on time, lower the interest rate on some debt a percentage or two by shopping around for a better rate, and skip a couple of restaurant meals — and it's possible to save $1,000. But instead, that money is going down the drain!

FIGURE 4-1

	A	B	C	D	E	F	G	H	I
1	**MONEY DRAIN PAIN**								
2									
3	How many hours a week do you work?							35	
4									
5	How many weeks of vacation do you take?							2	
6									
7	This is how many hours a year you work:							**1,750**	
8									
9	How much money are you wasting a year by ignoring your personal finances?							$1,000.00	
10									
11									
12							YOUR HOURLY PAY		Number of hours
13		Federal/Ontario	After-tax	Average	Marginal	Before	After	After	you are pouring
14	Taxable income	Tax	Income	Tax Rate	Tax Rate	Tax	Tax	Tax	down the drain
15							(Average)	(Marginal)	
16									
17	$5,000.00	$0.00	$5,000.00	0.00%	0.00%	$2.86	$2.86	$2.86	350
18	$10,000.00	$296.00	$9,704.00	2.96%	16.00%	$5.71	$5.55	$4.80	208
19	$15,000.00	$1,508.00	$13,492.00	10.05%	22.05%	$8.57	$7.71	$6.68	150
20	$20,000.00	$2,611.00	$17,389.00	13.06%	22.05%	$11.43	$9.94	$8.91	112
21	$25,000.00	$3,713.00	$21,287.00	14.85%	22.05%	$14.29	$12.16	$11.14	90
22	$30,000.00	$4,816.00	$25,184.00	16.05%	22.05%	$17.14	$14.39	$13.36	75
23	$35,000.00	$5,949.00	$29,051.00	17.00%	25.15%	$20.00	$16.60	$14.97	67
24	$40,000.00	$7,470.00	$32,530.00	18.68%	31.15%	$22.86	$18.59	$15.74	64
25	$45,000.00	$9,027.00	$35,973.00	20.06%	31.15%	$25.71	$20.56	$17.70	56
26	$50,000.00	$10,585.00	$39,415.00	21.17%	31.15%	$28.57	$22.52	$19.67	51
27	$55,000.00	$12,142.00	$42,858.00	22.08%	31.15%	$31.43	$24.49	$21.64	46
28	$60,000.00	$13,703.00	$46,297.00	22.84%	32.98%	$34.29	$26.46	$22.98	44
29	$65,000.00	$15,352.00	$49,648.00	23.62%	32.98%	$37.14	$28.37	$24.89	40
30	$70,000.00	$17,048.00	$52,952.00	24.35%	35.39%	$40.00	$30.26	$25.84	39
31	$75,000.00	$19,148.00	$55,852.00	25.53%	43.41%	$42.86	$31.92	$24.25	41
32	$80,000.00	$21,319.00	$58,681.00	26.65%	43.41%	$45.71	$33.53	$25.87	39
33	**$85,000.00**	**$23,489.00**	**$61,511.00**	**27.63%**	**43.41%**	**$48.57**	**$35.15**	**$27.49**	**36**
34	$90,000.00	$25,660.00	$64,340.00	28.51%	43.41%	$51.43	$36.77	$29.10	34
35	$95,000.00	$27,830.00	$67,170.00	29.29%	43.41%	$54.29	$38.38	$30.72	33
36	$100,000.00	$30,001.00	$69,999.00	30.00%	43.41%	$57.14	$40.00	$32.34	31
37	$105,000.00	$32,171.00	$72,829.00	30.64%	43.41%	$60.00	$41.62	$33.95	29
38	$110,000.00	$34,342.00	$75,658.00	31.22%	43.41%	$62.86	$43.23	$35.57	28
39	$115,000.00	$36,512.00	$78,488.00	31.75%	43.41%	$65.71	$44.85	$37.19	27
40	$120,000.00	$38,810.00	$81,190.00	32.34%	46.41%	$68.57	$46.39	$36.75	27
41	$125,000.00	$41,131.00	$83,869.00	32.90%	46.41%	$71.43	$47.93	$38.28	26
42	$130,000.00	$43,451.00	$86,549.00	33.42%	46.41%	$74.29	$49.46	$39.81	25
43	$135,000.00	$45,772.00	$89,228.00	33.91%	46.41%	$77.14	$50.99	$41.34	24
44	$140,000.00	$48,092.00	$91,908.00	34.35%	46.41%	$80.00	$52.52	$42.87	23
45	$145,000.00	$50,413.00	$94,587.00	34.77%	46.41%	$82.86	$54.05	$44.40	23
46	$150,000.00	$52,733.00	$97,267.00	35.16%	46.41%	$85.71	$55.58	$45.93	22
47	$155,000.00	$55,054.00	$99,946.00	35.52%	46.41%	$88.57	$57.11	$47.47	21
48	$160,000.00	$57,374.00	$102,626.00	35.86%	46.41%	$91.43	$58.64	$49.00	20
49	$165,000.00	$59,695.00	$105,305.00	36.18%	46.41%	$94.29	$60.17	$50.53	20
50	$170,000.00	$62,015.00	$107,985.00	36.48%	46.41%	$97.14	$61.71	$52.06	19
51	$175,000.00	$64,336.00	$110,664.00	36.76%	46.41%	$100.00	$63.24	$53.59	19

The spreadsheet shows how many hours a person would have to work at various income levels to leave enough money after tax to pay for this wasted $1,000. It begins with four simple questions. In Column H, I have entered sample answers to these questions as follows (but as with the other spreadsheets accompanying this workbook, you can enter your own data overtop of the sample data):

Number of hours worked per week: 35 (cell H3)

Weeks of vacation per year: 2 (cell H5)

- The number of hours per year worked is calculated for you in cell H7: 1,750 in this example

- The amount of money wasted each year: $1,000 (cell H9)

Directly under the questions is the table of results (A17 to I51), which are calculated as you enter your information. The annual salary of our test case is $85,000 a year, and this situation is described on line 33. In Ontario in 2005, this person would pay about $23,489 in Federal and Ontario income tax, leaving $61,511 after tax. (Check the updates page at Self-Counsel Press's website at <www.self-counsel.com> for additional spreadsheets with province-specific tax information.) This person's average tax rate is 27.63 percent (total tax divided by total income) but the marginal tax rate is 43.41 percent. This means that for every additional dollar this person earns, he or she loses $0.43 in taxes.

Now look at cell F33: the hourly rate of pay before tax is $48.57 ($85,000 divided by 1,750 hours). G33 shows the average hourly rate of pay after tax: $35.15 ($61,511 divided by 1,750 hours) in this case.

At the marginal rate of tax (43.41 percent), this person's after-tax rate is only $27.49 per hour (cell H33). That's the hourly rate before tax of $48.57 less 43.41 percent tax.

How many hours does this person need to work to pay for the wasted $1,000? The answer is 36. That's one full week of work.

Try it with your own numbers. Instead of $1,000 as a starting point in your own case, try a figure of 1 percent of your gross salary, say $500 if you earn $50,000 per year. Punch in your own numbers and see the positive effect plugging your money drains can have on your pocketbook ... and your life.

My Income and Expenses

Figure 4-2, My Income and Expenses, is a very straightforward spreadsheet that allows you to enter monthly information about your income and expenses in Column B. It subtotals all the amounts and also multiplies by 12 to give you the annual amounts in Column C, so there is no need to enter any information in Column C — the program does the calculation for you.

Other programs such as Intuit's Quicken or Microsoft Money will give you even more detail, but the My Income and Expenses spreadsheet will give you at least a rough idea of how much money you have coming in and where it's all going.

If you have expenses that are not listed on the spreadsheet, simply insert a row in the appropriate place for that expense — but be certain to create a formula for that row in Column C. The program will recalculate all the affected totals.

FIGURE 4-2 (1)

	A	B	C
		MONTH ($)	YEAR ($)
1	**MY INCOME AND EXPENSES**		
2	**Version 91105**		
3		MONTH ($)	YEAR ($)
4	**INCOME**		
5	My net pay		0.00
6	Self-employment income		0.00
7	Spouse's net pay		0.00
8	**TOTAL INCOME**	0.00	0.00
9	**EXPENSES**		
10	**Auto**		
11	Fuel		0.00
12	General		0.00
13	Insurance		0.00
14	Lease		0.00
15	License & registration		0.00
16	Loan interest		0.00
17	Maintenance		0.00
18	**Total auto**	0.00	0.00
19	**Business**		
20	Advertising		0.00
21	Auto fuel		0.00
22	Auto insurance		0.00
23	Auto lease		0.00
24	Auto loan interest		0.00
25	Auto maintenance		0.00
26	Auto parking		0.00
27	Auto other		0.00
28	Dues & subscriptions		0.00
29	Internet		0.00
30	Loan interest		0.00
31	Meals & entertainment		0.00
32	Office & general		0.00
33	**Total business**	0.00	0.00
34	**Children**		
35	Child care		0.00
36	Daycare		0.00
37	Holiday & camp programs		0.00
38	Lessons		0.00
39	Private school tuition		0.00
40	Trips & other		0.00
41	**Total children**	0.00	0.00
42	**Family**		
43	Cash withdrawals		0.00
44	Clothing		0.00
45	Donations		0.00
46	Entertainment		0.00
47	Gifts given		0.00
48	Groceries		0.00
49	Vacation		0.00
50	**Total family**	0.00	0.00

FIGURE 4-2 (2)

	A	B	C
51	**Household**		
52	Furniture		0.00
53	Insurance		0.00
54	Mortgage interest		0.00
55	Property tax		0.00
56	Repairs & maintenance		0.00
57	Rent		0.00
58	**Total household**	**0.00**	**0.00**
59	**Insurance**		
60	Disability		0.00
61	Life		0.00
62	Life--spouse		0.00
63	**Total insurance**	**0.00**	**0.00**
64	**Interest and bank charges**		
65	Bank charges		0.00
66	Credit card interest		0.00
67	Line of credit interest		0.00
68	Personal taxes interest		0.00
69	**Total interest and bank charges**	**0.00**	**0.00**
70	**Medical**		
71	Dental		0.00
72	Medical		0.00
73	Private health care		0.00
74	**Total medical**	**0.00**	**0.00**
75	**Other Expenses**		
76	Legal & professional fees		0.00
77	Recreation		0.00
78	Restaurant meals		0.00
79	RRSP admin fees		0.00
80	Subscriptions		0.00
81	Miscellaneous		0.00
82	**Total other expenses**	**0.00**	**0.00**
83	**Utilities**		
84	Cable TV		0.00
85	Cleaning		0.00
86	Electricity		0.00
87	Gas & oil		0.00
88	Lawn & driveway		0.00
89	Security		0.00
90	Telephone		0.00
91	Water		0.00
92	**Total utilities**	**0.00**	**0.00**
93	**TOTAL EXPENSES**	**0.00**	**0.00**
94	**INCOME LESS EXPENSES**	**0.00**	**0.00**

Cash Flow Projector

Another useful tool to help you gain control of your finances is the Cash Flow Projector (see Figure 4-3). It is designed to allow you to project your expenses for the entire year based on actual figures to a certain date. Here are the columns and what you need to enter:

- **Column B — Actual figures for the prior year:** These will come from your My Income and Expenses spreadsheet or your Quicken or Money cash flow reports.

- **Column C — Actual figures from January 1 to a certain date** (March 31 in this example): This is the actual money you earned and spent during the first quarter (or other period) of the current year.

- **Column D — Estimated figures since the date in Column C to December 31:** Here you should use the figures you entered in Column C to help you estimate what they will be for the rest of the year.

You don't need to enter any information into Column E. Column E contains formulas that automatically add the figures from Columns C and D to give you an estimate for the entire current year.

The Transfers section is where you should enter cash outflows that are not expenses, such as transfers to RRSPs and investment accounts or the payment of debt principal balances.

As always, feel free to change descriptions and add or take out lines as you see fit. If you add a line, be sure to create the formula in Column E for it.

FIGURE 4-3 (1)

	A	B	C	D	E
		Actual			Estimate
		20x1	1/1 - 3/31/20x2	4/1 - 12/31/20x2	20x2
1	CASH FLOW PROJECTOR				
2	Version 91105				
3					
4		Actual			Estimate
5		20x1	1/1 - 3/31/20x2	4/1 - 12/31/20x2	20x2
6					
7	INFLOWS				
8	Salary (gross)				0.00
9	Interest income				0.00
10	Other income				0.00
11	Salary of spouse (gross)				0.00
12	TOTAL INFLOWS	0.00	0.00	0.00	0.00
13	My tax				
14	CPP contributions				0.00
15	EI contributions				0.00
16	Income tax				0.00
17	Pension				0.00
18	Total my tax	0.00	0.00	0.00	0.00
19	Spouse's tax				
20	CPP contributions				0.00
21	EI contributions				0.00
22	Income tax				0.00
23	Pension				0.00
24	Total spouse's tax	0.00	0.00	0.00	0.00
25	Total tax	0.00	0.00	0.00	0.00
26					
27	My net pay	0.00	0.00	0.00	0.00
28	Spouse's net pay	0.00	0.00	0.00	0.00
29	Net other	0.00	0.00	0.00	0.00
30	NET INFLOWS	0.00	0.00	0.00	0.00
31					
32	EXPENSES				
33	Auto				
34	Fuel				0.00
35	General				0.00
36	Insurance				0.00
37	Lease				0.00
38	License & registration				0.00
39	Loan interest				0.00
40	Maintenance				0.00
41	Total auto	0.00	0.00	0.00	0.00

FIGURE 4-3 (2)

	A	B	C	D	E
42	**Business**				
43	Advertising				0.00
44	Auto fuel				0.00
45	Auto insurance				0.00
46	Auto lease				0.00
47	Auto loan interest				0.00
48	Auto maintenance				0.00
49	Auto parking				0.00
50	Auto other				0.00
51	Dues & subscriptions				0.00
52	Internet				0.00
53	Loan interest				0.00
54	Meals & entertainment				0.00
55	Office & general				0.00
56	**Total business**	0.00	0.00	0.00	**0.00**
57	**Children**				
58	Child care				0.00
59	Daycare				0.00
60	Holiday & camp programs				0.00
61	Lessons				0.00
62	Private school tuition				0.00
63	Trips & other				0.00
64	**Total children**	0.00	0.00	0.00	**0.00**
65	**Family**				
66	Cash withdrawals				0.00
67	Clothing				0.00
68	Donations				0.00
69	Entertainment				0.00
70	Gifts given				0.00
71	Groceries				0.00
72	Vacation				0.00
73	**Total family**	0.00	0.00	0.00	**0.00**
74	**Household**				
75	Furniture				0.00
76	Insurance				0.00
77	Mortgage interest				0.00
78	Property tax				0.00
79	Repairs & maintenance				0.00
80	Rent				0.00
81	**Total household**	0.00	0.00	0.00	**0.00**
82	**Insurance**				
83	Disability				0.00
84	Life				0.00
85	Life -- spouse				0.00
86	**Total insurance**	0.00	0.00	0.00	**0.00**
87	**Interest and bank charges**				
88	Bank charges				0.00
89	Credit card interest				0.00
90	Line of credit interest				0.00
91	Personal taxes interest				0.00
92	**Total interest and bank charges**	0.00	0.00	0.00	**0.00**

FIGURE 4-3 (3)

	A	B	C	D	E
93	**Medical**				
94	Dental				0.00
95	Medical				0.00
96	Private health care				0.00
97	**Total medical**	**0.00**	**0.00**	**0.00**	**0.00**
98	**Other Expenses**				
99	Legal & professional fees				0.00
100	Recreation				0.00
101	Restaurants -- personal meals				0.00
102	RRSP admin fees				0.00
103	Subscriptions				0.00
104	Miscellaneous				0.00
105	**Total other expenses**	**0.00**	**0.00**	**0.00**	**0.00**
106	**Utilities**				
107	Cable TV				0.00
108	Cleaning				0.00
109	Electricity				0.00
110	Gas & oil				0.00
111	Lawn & driveway				0.00
112	Security				0.00
113	Telephone				0.00
114	Water				0.00
115	**Total utilities**	**0.00**	**0.00**	**0.00**	**0.00**
116					
117	**TOTAL EXPENSES**	**0.00**	**0.00**	**0.00**	**0.00**
118					
119	**TRANSFERS**				
120	TO Mortgage	0.00	0.00	0.00	0.00
121	TO Investment a/c 1	0.00	0.00	0.00	0.00
122	TO Investment a/c 2	0.00	0.00	0.00	0.00
123	TO RESP	0.00	0.00	0.00	0.00
124	TO Business loan	0.00	0.00	0.00	0.00
125	TO My RRSP	0.00	0.00	0.00	0.00
126	TO Spouse's RRSP	0.00	0.00	0.00	0.00
127					
128	**TOTAL TRANSFERS**	**0.00**	**0.00**	**0.00**	**0.00**
129					
130	**TOTAL OUTFLOWS (Expenses + Transfers)**	**0.00**	**0.00**	**0.00**	**0.00**
131					
132	**NET INFLOWS LESS TOTAL OUTFLOWS**	**0.00**	**0.00**	**0.00**	**0.00**

Step 5

CARS: SHOULD I LEASE OR BUY?

Your choice of a car-ownership strategy can save you significant money. The key decision is whether it's better for you to lease or buy a car.

I must admit that for many years, I was totally against leasing. However, after careful consideration, I have slowly come to the realization that if certain variables are controlled, leasing can make sense.

To help you decide which option is right for you, I have written a spreadsheet I call the Car Lease versus Buy Analyzer.

This basic tool focuses on the central issue of the fixed costs of leasing versus buying. It does not address the issue of operating costs such as gas, oil, maintenance, and insurance; however, these costs are important and you need to think about them before you choose which car to buy. The spreadsheet is designed to consider the costs of leasing or buying the same model of car, so operating costs would be virtually the same and therefore won't impact this decision.

The Car Lease versus Buy Analyzer has five tabs: Home, Questions, Results, Assumption, and Loan. We'll be discussing each in turn. Like several of the other spreadsheets accompanying this workbook, I've created a sample case study on this one. It's the lease versus buy options for a luxury SUV. When you want to use the spreadsheet yourself, simply input your own information overtop of the sample data.

The Home Tab

Have a look at Figure 5-1, the Home tab of the spreadsheet. Just like the other calculators, this tab simply shows the version number (cell B2), some basic information, and links to the four other tabs.

FIGURE 5-1

	A	B	C	D	E	F	G	H	I	J	K	L	M	N	O
1	Car Lease versus Buy Analyzer														
2	Version	102005													
3															
4	Welcome, and don't worry. You don't have to be an Excel expert to use this spreadsheet!														
5															
6	All you need to do is answer the questions on the Questions tab and then go to the Results tab to discover whether you are better off leasing or buying a car.														
7															
8	Play with different scenarios and see which strategy is best for you!														
9															
10	INDEX (Click the words to go to the worksheets or click on the tabs below.)														
11		Questions													
12		Results													
13		Assumptions													
14		Loan													
15															
16	If you would like further information about how to simplify your finances, come and visit us at:														
17		Smokeandmirrors.ca													
18															
19	© Copyright 2005/2006 David Trahair, CA														

The Questions Tab

Figure 5-2 shows the Questions tab. The questions you'll find here are all easy-to-answer ones about the facts of a lease or car loan, such as down payment or upfront payment, loan or lease term, and interest rate. You may need to do a bit of homework before filling in the answers with your own information, but that shouldn't take you long.

FIGURE 5-2

	A	B	C	D	E	F	G	H	I	J	K	L
1	**Car Lease versus Buy Analyzer Questions**											
2												Your
3	Answer these questions in column L:											Answers
4												
5	GENERAL											
6		What is today's date?										10/20/2005
7		(i.e., 10/20/2005 or 20/10/2005)										
8												
9		What is your first and last name?										Dave Test
10		(i.e., Dave Test)										
11												
12		What car are you proposing to lease or buy?										Luxury SUV
13												
14	LEASE OPTION QUESTIONS											
15		What amount are you required to put down on the lease (including GST and PST)?										$9,822
16												
17		What amount of freight and PDI must you pay up front (including GST and PST)?										$1,926
18												
19		What is the monthly lease payment (including GST and PST)?										$573
20												
21		What is the term of the lease (in years)?										4
22												
23		What is the lease interest rate per year?										4.90%
24												
25		What is the end-of-lease option to purchase amount (including GST and PST)?										$27,500
26												
27	BUY OPTION QUESTIONS											
28		What is the purchase price of the car (including all taxes, delivery, freight)?										$59,656
29												
30		What amount will you put down on the purchase?										$11,748
31												
32		What is the annual interest rate on the car loan going to be?										4.90%
33												
34		How many years will you have the loan?										4

The questions are divided into categories as follows:

- General
- Lease Option Questions
- Buy Option Questions

Let's go through the answers to the questions in each section.

General

In Column L, I have entered the current date of October 20, 2005, the name Dave Test, and the type of car being purchased: Luxury SUV.

Lease option questions

In this section, I have entered the amount required as a deposit on the lease including taxes ($9,822), the amount of freight and pre-delivery inspection (PDI) including taxes ($1,926), the monthly lease payment including taxes ($573), as well as the term of the lease (4 years), the lease interest rate (4.9 percent), and the end-of-lease purchase option amount including taxes ($27,500).

Buy option questions

Here I have entered the purchase price of the car, including all taxes, delivery, and freight ($59,656) and the amount put down as a deposit ($11,748, which is the combined total required on the lease of $9,822 plus $1,926). (Note that I have kept the deposit in the buy option the same as in the leasing option since we are assuming the same amount of cash is available in both cases.) I have also entered the annual interest rate (4.9 percent) as well as the term of the loan (4 years).

Results

Figure 5-3 shows you the Results tab. As with some of the other spreadsheets accompanying this workbook, a summary of the inputs is shown in cells K4 to K21. The only new figure you'll notice is in cell K21. It's the monthly loan payment

FIGURE 5-3

Car Lease versus Buy Analyzer Results for: Dave Test

INPUT SUMMARY

Date this analysis was prepared:	10/20/2005
The car you are analyzing is:	Luxury SUV

LEASING

Amount you are required to put down on the lease (non-refundable, including tax):	$9,822
Amount of upfront freight, PDI, etc. (including tax):	$1,926
Monthly lease payment (including tax):	$573
The term of the lease in years:	4
Lease interest rate:	4.90%
End-of-lease purchase price	$27,500

BUY

The purchase price of the car (including all delivery, freight, and tax) is:	$59,656
Amount you are putting down against the purchase:	$11,748
The amount of the loan (purchase price less down payment) is:	$47,908
The annual interest rate on the car loan is:	4.90%
Number of years the loan is for:	4
Your monthly loan payment (principal & interest) is:	$1,101

Year	2005	2006	2007	2008	2009	2010	2011	2012	2013	2014	Total
Year #	1	2	3	4	5	6	7	8	9	10	(Yr 1 to 10)
LEASE											
Fixed Costs:											
Down payment	9,822										9,822
Freight, PDI, etc.	1,926										1,926
Lease payments	6,876	6,876	6,876	6,876							27,504
End-of-lease purchase	0	0	0	27,500							27,500
Total Fixed Costs	**$18,624**	**$6,876**	**$6,876**	**$34,376**	**$0**	**$0**	**$0**	**$0**	**$0**	**$0**	**$66,752**
Cost in today's money	$60,093										
BUY											
Fixed Costs:											
Down payment	11,748										11,748
Principal payments	11,113	11,670	12,255	12,869							47,907
Interest payments	2,100	1,543	958	344							4,945
Total Fixed Costs	**$24,961**	**$13,213**	**$13,213**	**$13,213**	**$0**	**$0**	**$0**	**$0**	**$0**	**$0**	**$64,600**
Cost in today's money	$60,280										
CASH OUTLAY DIFFERENCE	**-$6,337**	**-$6,337**	**-$6,337**	**$21,163**	**$0**	**$0**	**$0**	**$0**	**$0**	**$0**	**$2,152**

COST DIFFERENCE IN TODAY'S MONEY	
LEASE COSTS LESS	-$187

amount ($1,101), which is calculated on the Loan tab.

The table shown at A23 to N46 summarizes the annual lease and buy costs based on the input.

You'll note that in this example, the total lease costs (including the buyout amount) come to $66,752, and the total buy costs are $64,600, for a difference of $2,152. That's useful information, but to truly compare the lease versus buy costs, it's necessary to discount the future cash flows into today's dollars.

Discounting future cash flows means accounting for the fact that a dollar today is worth more than a dollar at a later time. For example, first think about interest earned on money in a bank account. If you could earn 5 percent a year in a bank account and you had $1 today, that dollar would be worth $1.05 a year from now, since it would grow by 5 percent. Discounting is the reverse of that. $1.05 that you have a year from now is worth $1 today when discounted at 5 percent. In other words, the present value of $1.05 received a year from now, discounted at 5 percent, is $1 in today's dollars.

The Analyzer spreadsheet discounts future cash flows for you (at a rate of 6 percent, as per the Assumptions tab, which is discussed below) in cells D32 for the lease and D40 for the buy option. As you can see, the lease total cost in today's dollars is $60,093 and for the buy option it's $60,280. The difference is only $187 — virtually insignificant.

Assumptions

Figure 5-4 shows the Assumptions tab. It lists the basic assumptions that have gone into building the Car Lease versus Buy Analyzer.

FIGURE 5-4

	A	B	C	D	E	F	G
1	**Car Lease versus Buy Analyzer Assumptions**						
2							
3	1. Loans are compounded on a monthly basis.						
4							
5	2. Loan payments are made at the end of the month.						
6							
7	3. After-tax rate of return of 6 percent on investments (opportunity cost).						

Loan

Figure 5-5 shows the Loan tab. On this tab, the program makes all the necessary calculations for the car loan based on the answers to the Buy Option Questions in the Questions tab.

Try It with Your Own Numbers

Try your own figures the next time you need to replace your existing car — before you sign on the dotted line.

FIGURE 5-5

Car Lease versus Buy Analyzer — Loan

	A	B	C	D	E	F	G	H
1	**Car Lease versus Buy Analyzer — Loan**							
2								
3	**Assumptions**			**Calculations**				
4	Original loan balance	$47,908.00		Original loan monthly payment			$1,101.12	4
5	Loan annual interest rate	4.90%		Annual payment for loan			$13,213.42	
6	Term (years)	4		Term (years)			4.00	
7	Term (months)	48		Term (months)			48.00	
8								
9	Note: Interest compounds monthly, payments at end of period							
10								
11	Loan amortization schedule		Loan Principal Balance	Loan Principal Balance (Formatted)	Interest Payments	Principal Payments	Total Payments	
12								
13								
14								
15		Year						
16	1	2005	-$36,794.69	$36,794.69	$2,100.11	$11,113.31	$13,213.42	
17	2	2006	-$25,124.42	$25,124.42	$1,543.16	$11,670.26	$13,213.42	
18	3	2007	-$12,869.30	$12,869.30	$958.30	$12,255.13	$13,213.42	
19	4	2008	$0.00	$0.00	$344.12	$12,869.30	$13,213.42	
20	5	2009	$0.00	$0.00	$0.00	$0.00	$0.00	
21	6	2010	$0.00	$0.00	$0.00	$0.00	$0.00	
22	7	2011	$0.00	$0.00	$0.00	$0.00	$0.00	
23	8	2012	$0.00	$0.00	$0.00	$0.00	$0.00	
24	9	2013	$0.00	$0.00	$0.00	$0.00	$0.00	
25	10	2014	$0.00	$0.00	$0.00	$0.00	$0.00	
26	11	2015	$0.00	$0.00	$0.00	$0.00	$0.00	
27	12	2016	$0.00	$0.00	$0.00	$0.00	$0.00	
28	13	2017	$0.00	$0.00				
29	14	2018	$0.00	$0.00				
30	15	2019	$0.00	$0.00				
31	16	2020	$0.00	$0.00				
32	17	2021	$0.00	$0.00				
33	18	2022	$0.00	$0.00				
34	19	2023	$0.00	$0.00				
35	20	2024	$0.00	$0.00				
36	21	2025	$0.00	$0.00				
37	22	2026	$0.00	$0.00				
38	23	2027	$0.00	$0.00				
39	24	2028	$0.00	$0.00				
40	25	2029	$0.00	$0.00				

APPENDIX

Memo to: My broker

Subject: Problems with your service

Date: _____, 20__

I have been meaning to send you this memo for some time because we have become increasingly dissatisfied with the service you and your firm have been providing. I have separated the issues into three categories of concern. As you will see, some of the points are comments, and some require an answer from you.

Statements

- **Lack of information:** Investment statements do not show the following for each of our accounts:

  i) Rate of return information for each account for year-to-date, annual, 3 years, 5 years, and since inception

  ii) Rate of return information for each investment in each account for the same periods as above

- **Asset allocation:** Your firm has never prepared a consolidated summary of all our accounts of our investments by type (i.e., fixed income, low-risk equities, high-risk equities, labour-sponsored funds, income trusts, etc.). We want to receive one immediately. Such a summary should also include rate-of-return information by type so that a comparison to industry benchmarks can be made. We feel this information is essential for effective investment decision making.

- **Statement format:** Printing summary account information to page two rather than page one so that only contact information is visible on the first page is not only annoying, it's also a waste of paper. Please discontinue this practice.

- **Statement frequency:** Mailing statements only when there is activity in the cash account is senseless. We need monthly statements to stay informed of our investments' performance.

Fees

- **Hidden charges:** We have become aware of the extensive fees we are being charged behind the scenes by the mutual fund companies only through articles written by independent newspapers, including the excellent reports by the *Globe and Mail*. These fees, while not visible on our statements, are eating away at our returns. Again, we have become aware of alternatives such as exchange-traded funds and F-class mutual funds only through our own research. Isn't there supposed to be full disclosure of all fees we are paying?

    We want a summary, beginning as at the date we started investing with you, of all fees paid on our investments in each of our accounts from all the fund companies, as well as any other fees not listed on our monthly statements.

- **Deferred Sales Charges (DSC):** While we were aware that a sliding scale commission would be charged if mutual funds are cashed in before the required time, we personally feel "locked in" on many funds that are performing poorly. Full disclosure of the percentage and dollar amount of the redemption fee each year should be provided before any purchase is authorized. We will no longer be purchasing any DSC funds. Our decision now will be a difficult one: cash out and pay the fees or hang on and hope things get better. In both cases, we will probably lose.

- **Administration charges:** You charge an annual "administration fee" of $200 or so and encourage us to pay it from funds outside our investment accounts to avoid eating away at our RRSPs. However, hidden fees such as those buried in the management expenses (MERs) of the mutual funds we invest in take huge bites out of our RRSPs. This is particularly irritating. We request that this fee be waived on all our accounts from now on, as is the practice with other brokerage firms.

Rate of return

- Our overall rate of return on all our investments has been ____ percent per annum since _____. This return is approximately ___ percent less than the average 5-year GIC return for the same period.

- Going forward, we will be switching to fixed-income and low-fee, low-risk equity products and encouraging others to do the same.

    This is about my family's future. We simply can't afford to continue with the status quo.